Reflecting
Children's
Lives

Reflecting Children's Lives

A Handbook
for Planning Child-Centered Curriculum

Deb Curtis and Margie Carter

Redleaf Press

Illustrations by: Morning Glory Design
                         Saint Peter, MN

Published by: Redleaf Press
                         a division of Resources for Child Caring
                         450 North Syndicate, Suite 5
                         Saint Paul, MN 55104

Distributed by: Gryphon House
                         P.O. Box 207
                         Beltsville, MD 20704-0207

Library of Congress Cataloging-in-Publication Data

Curtis, Deb.
      Reflecting children's lives : a handbook for planning child-centered
curriculum / Deb Curtis, Margie Carter
              p.   cm.
      Included bibliographical references (p. 191),
      ISBN 1-884834-27-2
      1. Early childhood education--Curricula.   2. Curriculum planning.
      3. Classroom environment.   I. Carter, Margie. II. Title.
LB1139.4.C88 1996
375'.001--dc20   96-41080
                                                    CIP

Dedication

Reflecting Children's Lives: A Handbook for Planning Child-Centered Curriculum *is dedicated to Elizabeth Jones, who has made a tremendous contribution to our thinking and practice, and to the advancement of our profession. Betty keeps us observing, talking, re-examining, writing, and, of course, playing. We take inspiration from who she is and what she does. With gratitude, we follow in her path.*

And to Marian Wright Edelman, a prophet for our time and a remarkably fierce guardian of childhood. Though we don't know her personally, she inspires us to take risks and fight for what we know to be true. When we are tired or discouraged, her work both humbles and rejuvenates us.

Thanks to Jim Greenman who first put the phrase "creating places for childhood" in our heads; to Mary Steiner Whelan and Rosemary Wallner for their fine editorial suggestions; and to Morning Glory Design for translating our ideas into illustrations and a visually pleasing design.

Most of all we are grateful to our sons, Casey and Peter, who deepened our understanding of childhood and fueled our passion to preserve this precious time of life.

Contents

Introduction

Chapter 1

Begin with Yourself

Chapter 2

Revitalizing the Environment

Chapter 3

Putting the Child Back in DAP

Chapter 4

Redefining Curriculum Themes

Chapter 5

Caring for Infants and Toddlers

Chapter 6

Organizing and Communicating Your Approach
to Curriculum Planning

Chapter 7

Developing Yourself

Recommended Resources

Introduction

Across the United States and Canada, and in many other countries around the world, members of the early childhood care and education profession are hard at work creating programs for young children. Increasingly, this involves planning for young ones who will spend an estimated 12,000 hours of their childhood in group care and institutional settings. Millions of children spend the waking hours of their childhood not with their families or in their neighborhoods, but in settings centered around schedules, health and safety concerns, and the constraints of what adults can do with large groups of children.

Few of us who provide this full-time care and education experienced it ourselves as children. A camp or school model is the only positive picture we have of group care. This image strongly influences how we think about curriculum planning. Another influence is the lack of credence and recognition the general public gives to our work, leading us to bolster our self-image with what we think are "real teacher" behaviors and lesson plans.

Around us are those concerned about the lack of success many children have in school and the highly competitive job market they will face in the future. While many early childhood professionals share these concerns, we have, perhaps, a different understanding about what children need to thrive in school and life. Many parents, government, and school policy makers press for an increasingly earlier emphasis on academic success. Misguidedly, they think this means more tightly prescribed programs, learning outcomes, and assessment tools for younger and younger children.

With a different vision, early childhood educators are inventing this work as we go. Fortunately, our profession is identifying resources and curriculum approaches to keep us focused on the cultural and developmental needs of young children. There is an explosion of interest in anti-bias practices, emergent curriculum and the project approach. We have models such as Bank Street, the Creative Curriculum, High/Scope, Waldorf, Montessori, and the schools of Reggio Emilia in Italy. Each of these has something to offer us in our efforts to create programs for real childhoods, but we should be wary of anything that suggests a perfect recipe for the complex cauldron of working with young children.

For our curriculum planning to be relevant and reflect the needs of children, we should pay close attention to the children themselves and to the economic and ideological interests that compete for their childhoods. We must continue to develop ourselves as competent caregivers and teachers. Simultaneously, our task is to become advocates, strong voices, and activists on behalf of children, their needs, and ours. Getting better at what we do involves taking a close look at ourselves. It means making changes, taking risks, and building systems for collaboration and support. Like children, teachers and caregivers are engaged in a developmental process. You will find stories to that effect in many of these chapters. For inspiration and a vision of where you might travel on this journey, consider reading these stories with your co-workers or classmates.

This handbook was developed to help you on your professional journey. It is primarily focused on planning for preschool children, but includes a section for those who work with infants and toddlers. You may encounter this book as a text for a class you are taking. Or you may discover it as a resource for curriculum planning for yourself or others you are mentoring. Teachers, education coordinators, directors, and college instructors will find ideas and strategies here to help create, in early childhood program designer and author Jim Greenman's words, "places for childhoods."

What You'll Discover

As you look through this handbook, you'll discover activities for both you and the children. It is designed to help you chart your own thinking as you consider new possibilities for your curriculum planning.

Chapter 1 begins with self-assessment activities. Whenever you set about learning something new, begin with what you already know and feel. Use the checklists, comparative charts, and questions to make note of your present knowledge and experiences before you move through the next chapters. These notes will give you a reference for considering what you want to learn from the following pages.

The foundation of curriculum planning and child guidance is the learning environment. In chapter 2, you'll look at the environment you are providing. This chapter includes quick checklists for assessing your current environment for key elements of childhood: cultivating dreams and imagination, reflecting real lives, and providing for physical power and adventure. There are suggestions for your space, schedule, and classroom routines, along with lists of open-ended materials that help you create a "loose parts" curriculum. This chapter ends with an inspiring story of how one program used these ideas to create an outdoor play space.

As you plan a child-centered and developmentally appropriate environment, chapter 3 emphasizes the importance of observation. You'll find self-directed activities to guide you in strengthening your observation skills and a form to copy for your ongoing use. Journal entries from a teacher learning to base her curriculum on observations of children end this chapter.

In chapter 4, you'll reconsider your approach to theme planning. There are activities to remind you of the stages of play as defined by Piaget, followed by suggestions of materials that will enhance your ability to provide for the themes of meaningful work, physical development, creative expression, transformation activities, and learning skills. You'll find children's projects to analyze and teacher responses to consider. The chapter closes with a story of a master teacher whose deep respect for children leads to an extensive curriculum project based on their passion for fairness.

Curriculum for infants and toddlers must be centered around building relationships, which is the focus of chapter 5. Building relationships involves knowing the developmental themes of this time of life and reading cues with the response of an improvisational artist. You'll find a story here describing this response as "riding the waves."

Chapter 6 will help you organize and communicate your approach to child-centered curriculum planning. You'll find several possible schema to help you begin to break out of the tiny boxes of a weekly schedule that usually record your curriculum and examples of forms other professionals have used. Completing the self-directed activities will help you to strengthen your ability to communicate the value of what you are doing. Three stories round out this chapter: one from a kindergarten teacher, one from a head start program, and one from a child development center on a military base.

For further consideration of your professional journey, chapter 7 includes new ways to think about the roles you play with children, dispositions to cultivate in yourself, and ways to enhance your own sense of wonder and aesthetics. Also included are a self-assessment checklist and a teacher's story of narrating her self-discovery as she works with children.

At the end of the handbook, you'll find a "Recommended Resources" section to continue your professional journey and build on the ideas presented in this handbook. This list is not intended to be all inclusive, but rather a sharing of sources that have continued to contribute to our thinking and practice.

A Work in Progress

Think of *Reflecting Children's Lives* as your work in progress. Use the spaces provided on many pages to take notes and record a question, a memory of a related experience or idea, or something you need help with. Go through this handbook at your own pace, alone or with colleagues. Take the time to complete the suggested activities and make note of things you already know and things you still don't understand. Use this as a workbook that you return to for inspiration and ideas. See it as a record of the development of your own thinking and practice.

You may recognize some ideas on these pages from other books we or our colleagues have written. They appear here as strategies for planning curriculum for your children and for setting goals for your professional growth. Draw on this handbook when you need to rethink what you're doing, or when you're planning workshops and classes. Use it to help you coach new teachers, volunteers, substitutes, or parents in your classroom. Use it to enhance your ability to stand for children and to speak up for the childhood they need to be really ready for school and a successful life.

Begin with Yourself

Could

one of these

teachers

be you?

1

Verna is a positive, upbeat teacher. She loves children and conscientiously pursues her curriculum goals, following the latest information available to preschool teachers. She continually tries out new activities from curriculum books. Verna has her ups and downs but says her classroom runs well. Increasingly, however, she's unsettled, with nagging doubts about her teaching. Many of the activities she plans don't seem very meaningful to the children. A small voice inside her triggers closer examination and questions about what's going on. **Isabel** has been a family provider for two years. She offers a relaxed home environment with a variety of toys for the children to play with. She believes in letting kids do what they want. During the last few months, however, Isabel finds herself turning on the television more often, trying to keep the kids from fighting and getting too wound up. She's saving money to buy some new toys and thinks she'll get some worksheets and craft books to try to keep the kids busy. **Michael** teaches in a government-funded preschool program. Much of his time is spent completing paperwork—forms, reports, lesson plans, and assessments. He diligently tries to make his classroom reflect the standards and regulations that are requirements of his job. His time with children is orderly and smooth because he is very organized and skilled at group management. Recently he's begun to feel like something is missing in his work life. When he's honest with himself, he admits he isn't building real relationships with the children. He doesn't know what essential answers all of the paperwork is about. He's just going through all of the motions.

Welcome to the Journey

Opening this handbook reveals a journey many providers and teachers are on—searching for a curriculum that is more alive and meaningful for the children and themselves. As you join in this search, you have probably begun to challenge yourself to look thoughtfully and with new eyes at what is happening in your classroom. Let's see what you will discover.

Read through the list at right and check what's true for you.

- Have you asked yourself why you plan curriculum the way you do?
  - ☐ Do you follow the same daily routines and curriculum plans because this is the way you've always done it?
  - ☐ Do you obediently follow rules and regulations, not knowing or questioning the reasons why these exist?
  - ☐ Have you noticed that the children are restless and bored, and so are you?
  - ☐ Does life in your program reflect what you and the children really care about?

- Is your work life stressful and fast-paced, your time filled with a continuous cycle of activity preparation and cleanup; parent notes, lesson plans, reports, and newsletters to write; memos, notices, new regulations, and articles to read?
  - ☐ Do you have limited opportunity to slow down and spend quality time with children?
  - ☐ Are you exhausted at the end of each day, more because of what didn't happen with the kids than because of what did?

- Are you concerned because your program has been invaded by commercialism and the media's idea of childhood? Do children's toys, lunch boxes, and clothes reflect the latest superhero products from TV and movies?

  ☐ Do you find the children following the scripts of these violent and stereotyped characters with play that is repetitive and lacking in creativity?

  ☐ Do most of your interactions with children involve stopping fights or soothing hurt feelings?

  ☐ Have you noticed that many toys are designed and packaged with predetermined themes and limited opportunity for investigation, invention, or using one's own ideas or imagination?

  ☐ Are you concerned because when you provide open-ended, more challenging activities and toys the children don't know how to begin without your help and some are even reluctant to try?

- Do you ever feel it's time to re-examine the icons of preschool culture: circle time, calendar time, cleanup time, paper plate and paper bag art projects, holiday themes, the value of learning the ABC song?

  ☐ Do your holiday projects create additional stress and exhaustion for you and children and convey an underlying message of commercialism?

  ☐ Have any children in your program been overlooked because you assumed all families celebrate and value traditional Christian or European-American based holidays?

  ☐ Have you discovered that getting children ready for kindergarten often really means "Now I know my ABCs, and they don't mean a thing to me"?

The three Rs aren't enough

Literature and research in the early childhood profession tell us that children thrive when they have real relationships. They grow when curriculum activities are meaningful and geared to their interests and developmental and cultural needs. They develop positive self-esteem, social skills, and confidence when their family life and culture are part of the life of the classroom.

At the heart of children's learning is active play—uninterrupted time to explore, be physically competent, and represent their experience and understandings.

Yet, an emphasis on "school readiness" suggests play and other aspects of childhood are foolish, immature, and something to outgrow. This emphasis leads to a preschool curriculum that is abstract, and often includes meaningless memorization and parroting. A simplified version of the "Three Rs" doesn't capture children's imaginations or engage their minds. It leads to behavior problems and teacher burnout.

There are, however, more significant and satisfying "Rs" for children and teachers to learn. We've listed a few of our favorites on the next page.

More R's to Learn

Remember to slow down. Take time to really notice and delight in children and the magic of their development.

Reawaken yourself and the children to a sense of wonder, curiosity, a passion for discovery, and new learning.

Re-evaluate your goals and focus your curriculum on relationships with people, nature, and the learning process.

Recognize that childhood is a time for intense intellectual pursuit and social and emotional learning. Build curriculum on children's interests, and on the questions and skills they are pursuing.

Respond to children's need for time. Provide opportunities to investigate and practice a skill over and over again. Extended, engaged activity helps children deepen their understandings and build confidence in their abilities and ideas. Taking time to explore and express oneself nourishes a love for learning.

Refocus your celebrations on meaningful events and accomplishments that occur as a part of the daily life of your classroom. Create rituals and representations to help everyone pay attention to the miracles of life, the joys of discovery, and the community we can create together.

Reinforce collaboration rather than competition. Provide activities, experiences, and materials that encourage working together rather than working in isolation.

Reconnect with your community. Plan the majority of activities in your curriculum around real people, real issues, and real work needing to be done.

Represent the interests, activities, and thinking process that is the heart of your program. Take time to observe, record, and create displays with photos, stories, and celebrations honoring the events in your daily lives together.

Renew yourself often! Take regular time for self-reflection and self-care and for collaborative thinking and work with friends and colleagues. You can't care for others if you haven't taken care of yourself.

Revive your activism on behalf of children and yourself. Children need us to champion the importance of childhood and the value of play, joyful discovery, and feeling alive in our body. The early childhood profession needs advocates for recognition, respect, and adequate compensation for the valuable work we do.

Adding these "Rs" into your work does not mean adding more stress to your already busy life. Rather, it implies slowing down and building from what's already available within and around you, in the children, families, and community. It only requires that you observe carefully, think critically, and cultivate your own passion for childhood.

How do the Children Feel?

The focus of emergent curriculum is on the children and their needs. As you read through this chart, think about what these concepts would mean to the children in your class. Which approach would excite them? Which would get them to participate and open up to you?

Traditional Approaches	Child-Centered Approaches
Teachers believe the primary purpose of preschool is to give children a head start on academic lessons.	Teachers put play at the heart of the curriculum. They provide for play with ample time and materials.
Teacher planning is focused only on group times and art projects, neglecting regular changes to the environment to continually add new curiosity and possibilities.	Teachers plan the environment as the basis for the curriculum, which is child-centered and reflects the children's interests and lives. Materials are in good condition, interesting, and organized with attention to aesthetics.
Curriculum activities are focused on dittos, art products, and topical themes presented to children during group time. These materials make sure children have work to take home as a demonstration of what they are learning in preschool.	Teachers understand that children are active, sensory learners who need many opportunities for self-chosen exploration, social interaction, and problem-solving. These teachers are more interested in this process than in final products to show off the curriculum.
Teachers ignore most nondisruptive, child-initiated play. Instead, they do housekeeping and record-keeping tasks during "free choice time"; they view free play as a break from the curriculum.	Teachers observe individual children and the themes of their physical, cognitive, social, and emotional development. They make note of the children's questions, skills, and frustrations.

Traditional Approaches	Child-Centered Approaches
Teacher-directed curriculum themes overshadow or hide children's interests. Look-alike products are displayed on the bulletin boards with no sign of children's imaginations or interests.	Teachers use children's "themes" as the basis for curriculum planning. Planning involves an introduction of materials and interactions to stimulate the emergence of the children's ideas and understandings.
Teachers police the room, keeping children on task, regulating the use of materials, and disciplining children who haven't learned social skills.	As the children engage with materials provided, teachers observe, offer guidance, and plan enrichment activities to add to the environment.
Teachers base their plans around traditional school topics, popular culture holidays, and pre-packaged seasonal curriculum theme books.	Teachers share their own passions, interests, and questions, which may serve as another source of children's interests and curriculum.
Curriculum plans are pulled from files and activity books and are repeated on an annual basis as "topics to be covered."	Written curriculum plans document the children's involvement with materials, questions, and discoveries, rather than document activities teachers will direct.
Teachers focus their individual planning for children on academic deficiencies and the need for repetitive practice of the school readiness skills the children have yet to acquire.	For typically developing children, individual planning addresses frustrations by focusing on children's strengths. Teachers seek the child's point of view in pursuing any readiness agenda.

Read through the chart again. This time, think about your approach to curriculum. What activities, finger plays, room decorations, and role plays have you planned that utilize the traditional approach? What have you tried (or would like to try) that would foster and encourage the child-centered approach?

Analyzing Curriculum Plans

Melissa's October Curriculum

Now that you know there is more to the "Three Rs" and have thought about curriculum from a child's point of view, read through the following October curriculums. Melissa's and Sharon's plans reflect two very different ways of thinking about curriculum activities for young children. As you read through each one, analyze each teacher's approach. To help you, keep the following questions in mind.

- What teacher goals do these curriculum plans suggest?
- How does the teacher think the children learn?
- What are the sensory aspects of this curriculum?
- What values are promoted (consider religious, commercial, diversity)?
- How do these curriculum plans draw on the children's daily lives and experiences?

Themes: Scary things (witches, bats, black cats, spiders), trick- or-treat, costumes

Room Environment: Commercial cutouts: jack-o'-lanterns, witches, skeletons; spider webs hanging on wall; children's complete Halloween art projects

Art Projects:
- Paper plate pumpkins: paint plates orange and paste on black face shapes

- Construction paper spiders: attach pre-cut legs to body and hang
- Scary night: crayon drawings of "spooky" pictures sponged with black
- Ghost print: use white tempera on black construction paper
- Stand-up pumpkins: glue colored pumpkin dittos on cardboard
- Trick-or-treat bags: Halloween-shape cutouts glued on paper bags
- Pumpkin accordion people: accordion-fold strips glued on body parts of pumpkin-head people
- Egg carton witch: egg carton sections decorated as witches with collage materials and pre-cut face pieces to glue on

Games and Movement Activities:
- The old witch and the cat: one child is the witch; the others sit in a circle and are cats; the witch hobbles around the circle with a blindfold; one of the cats meow; the witch tries to guess who that child is
- Spiders and flies: tag game with some children as flies, some as spiders
- Ghost, ghost, witch: a variation of duck, duck, goose
- Jack-o'-lantern bean bag throw: throw bean bags through holes

Poems and Songs: "Halloween Time"; "Five Little Ghosts"; "Five Little Jack-o'-Lanterns"; "How Does a Goblin Go?"; "Cackle, Cackle, Ugly Witch"

Books: Little Witches Halloween Book; The Tooth Witch; The Halloween Party; Scary, Scary Halloween; Ghost's Hour, Spook Hour

Special Activities:
- Carving pumpkin: children help teacher decide what kind of jack-o'-lantern face to have on a pumpkin and watch while it is carved

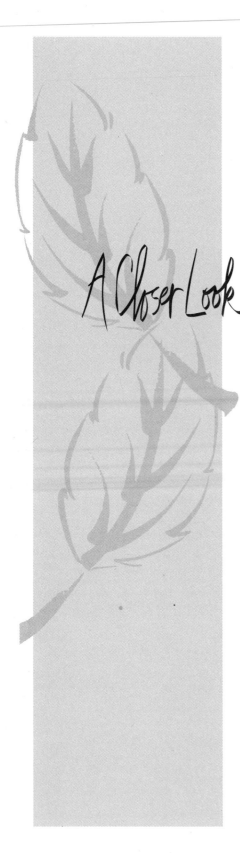

A Closer Look

- Halloween party: children wear costumes from home (Indian, Batman, Power Ranger, Barbie, princess, bride, etc.); trick-or-treat within program classrooms; jack-o'-lantern cupcakes, witch's brew and Halloween candy as party treats
- Cooking projects: spooky gelatin spiders; monster toast; witch's brew; jack-o'-lantern fruit cup

Melissa's October curriculum is probably familiar to most of us as it centers around the traditional practice of using commercialized, European-American holidays as the focus for planning.

In this approach, children are consumers of activities and images rather than inventors. Melissa offers pre-planned, pre-made, and simplistic projects. She overlooks the opportunity to have the children explore their own understandings and underlying rationale for the project. There is no "real" connection to their lives as children; there is even less sensory exploration or active participation.

Most teachers argue that children love Halloween. Upon closer examination, however, we can see that children really don't love commercialized cuteness, or stereotypical costumes, or being frightened. What they do love is the magic and drama that comes with make-believe play and dress-up. They love the power of acting out a role and the surprise of transforming themselves and the world around them.

With these ideas in mind, analyze another October curriculum using the same questions as mentioned at the beginning of this section.

Sharon's October Curriculum

Themes: Autumn harvest, end of the growing season (death); surprise, transforming materials, masks, dress-up, role-play

Room Environment:
- Objects from outdoors: dead vines and leaves, pinecones, gourds, pumpkins, nuts, bones
- Rotting and molding pumpkin: magnifying glass; small container for composting to watch decaying process
- Photographs of children: on field trips to pumpkin farm and apple orchard
- Children's dictation: stories of their experiences on the field trips and in the classroom
- Display table honoring people and pets who have died: photographs from home, dictated stories

Sensory and Cooking Activities:
- Pumpkin cutting: children each help cut their own pumpkin; explore the seeds, texture, smell, taste
- Roasting and tasting pumpkin seeds
- Baking pumpkin pie and custard
- Peeling, coring, and washing apples
- Making applesauce
- Tasting and comparing different kinds of apples
- Harvesting and drying: apples, herbs, and flowers
- Making and drinking: mint, chamomile, and ginger teas
- Grinding and tasting: spices such as cinnamon, nutmeg, and cloves
- Making and eating soups such as pumpkin, squash, potato, and vegetable
- Making and mixing: magic brews of food color and water; oil and water; cornstarch and water; baking soda and vinegar
- Enhancing the sensory table: pinecones, leaves, cinnamon sticks, dried flowers, mint, and nuts
- Cracking and eating: nuts
- Smelling and kneading: black playdough scented with spices of cloves, cinnamon, vanilla, almond, peppermint extracts; some with glitter

Classification and Sorting: Variety of apples, squashes, seeds, nuts, leaves, pinecones, herbs, flowers to sort and classify

Dramatic Play and Dress-Up:
- Prop boxes: a variety of fabrics, scarves, hats, jewelry, shoes, capes, wands, and pouches; children create their own costumes and dramatic play roles
- Face painting: use non-toxic face paints; include mirrors, camera, related books about fiestas, carnivals
- Warm clothes: mittens, hats, afghans, and boots in house corner

Art Activities: Collage materials: papier-mâché to make masks; glitter, feathers, fabric, paper scraps; full range of paint colors; drawing and cutting implements; a variety of ways to attach things together (including glue, stapler, tape, hole punches, brads, yarn, and rings)

Music and Movement:
Play music (classical, blues, nature sounds); harvest and fall songs; move like animals, the weather, leaves, trees; dance with scarves and feathers.

Books: The Pumpkin Seed; The Little Old Lady Who Was Not Afraid of Anything; The Barn Dance; Rain Makes Applesauce; All For Fall; Frederick; Lifetimes; The Tenth Good Thing About Barney; Pablo Remembers; To Hell With Dying; The Moon Was at a Fiesta; Tonight Is Carnaval; science and nature books; children's dictated stories made into books.

Special Activities and Field Trips: Take trips to pumpkin patch and apple orchard to get food for cooking.

As autumn arrives, Sharon knows children's senses are aroused in response to the changes they notice. Her October curriculum reflects the concrete and sensory aspects of children's daily experiences. She plans ways for them to explore and learn more about what they can see, hear, and smell all around them.

Sharon provides materials and activities that fully engage children's bodies and senses. She offers opportunities for exploration and observation of the more important themes of trying on new roles, being powerful, life and death, transformation of materials, nature and people. Sharon has planned fully for process and investigation, rather than products and clichés. The children are creators of this curriculum.

A Closer Look

About Your Current

Approach to

Curriculum Planning

*Use this space
to reflect
on your approach
to curriculum
planning.
These questions
will get you
started.*

When I plan my curriculum, what tends to be my focus?

What can I say about the complexity and meaning of the activities I provide?

How could I improve my present curriculum, using the information from this chapter?

Revitalizing the Environment

The environment is
the foundation of
the early childhood
curriculum.

2

Think about your home. What rooms do you feel most comfortable in? What elements and objects reflect who you are, what you care about, your history and interests? What are you drawn to because of its beauty? **What gives you the most pleasure** to look at, touch, listen to?

Environments

Beyond the Basics

Our environments have a great influence on how we feel and behave and what we pay attention to. This is especially true for children in our early childhood program environments. If children are spending the waking hours of their childhoods in disorganized, unattractive places, this climate will impact what they are learning, how they behave, and who they become.

The environment is the foundation of any early childhood curriculum. Most early childhood books on environments describe the basics of organizing a preschool classroom: defined activity areas and age-appropriate materials that are visible and accessible on low shelving. Although these basics are important for a child-centered curriculum, quality places for childhood go beyond these basics. The environment should also be intriguing and aesthetically pleasing. It should be inviting and cultivate children's curiosity and imagination.

Take the Child's Point of View

Take a minute to examine your preschool environment. Does it go beyond clean and orderly to encourage curiosity and joy? Get down on your knees and look at it from a child's point of view. Are things of interest within your reach? Are there things you are curious about and want to touch and investigate? If your friends came here to play with you, would there be enough room? Can you find things to use as props in your play? Do you see things that make you feel at home?

As you're down on your knees in your classroom, looking at things from a child's perspective, read through the following checklist. Mark the things that are true about your environment.

- Materials are visible, accessible, aesthetically organized, and attractive to children.
- Diverse textures, shapes, and elements of the natural world are present to invite exploration and discovery.
- The space is flexible, allowing for expansion when many children are working in the same area. There are minimal restrictions to moving in and out of areas.
- In addition to specialized toys such as pretend food, wooden blocks, and Lego building blocks, there is an ample supply of "loose parts": open-ended materials such as large pieces of fabric, corks, tubes, and plastic rings.
- Children's lives and interests are represented throughout the room; there are work samples, photos, sketches, and objects with stories.
- Visual images represent a range of roles and cultural expressions to learn about similarities and differences.

Now review the list. How many points have check marks by them? Not too many? Most of them? Are you surprised at the results? Read the following sections for strategies that will help you create an environment where both you and the children will love to spend time.

Cultivate

Dreams and Imagination

Begin enriching environments for children (and ourselves) by paying attention to aesthetics and wonder. Consider the typical classroom: bright, primary colors; cute cartoon drawings and commercial characters on the displays and toys; and materials made of plastic and other synthetics.

This environment may be utilitarian and easy to stock, but what does it say about our values? A typical preschool environment is overstimulating, rather than provoking children's curiosity or imagination. The room feels more commercial than inviting, cozy, or filled with natural wonders to explore.

As you look around your room and think about making it more inviting and aesthetically pleasing, consider the three important elements of storage, lighting, and decoration.

First, thoughtful storage and display of materials will convey a natural sense of order as well as beauty. Accessible storage invites children's curiosity and encourages them to appreciate and use materials more intentionally. Here are ideas to keep in mind.

Ideas for Storage

- Use storage containers made of interesting textures.
- Arrange furniture, materials, and wall decorations with an eye on balance and design.
- Easy-to-find storage and display ideas include: straw baskets; wooden bowls; trays with designs

and patterns; clear plastic tubs and boxes; decorated jars, boxes and tubs; hat boxes, decorated cartons and boxes; mirrors (all sizes and shapes) in unexpected places around the room to help children see themselves and others from different perspectives.

Second, pay close attention to the lighting in your environment. Thoughtful use of light and shadows can awaken children to new perspectives, enchantment and excitement about learning. Consider the following.

Ideas for Lighting

- Whenever possible, have natural light in your classroom.
- Hang things in windows that blow in the breeze, create rainbows, and cast shadows in the room.
- Use safety lamps, dimmer switches, and other sources of indirect lighting throughout the environment. In some places, use colored lightbulbs or theater gel to highlight areas or create special moods.
- Light candles (in enclosed containers and out of children's reach) for meals and naptime to signal special times and rituals of the day.
- Place mirrors on walls, shelves, and counters to reflect light and images and create a spacious feeling.

Ideas for Softness and Pleasure

Third, at garage sales, flea markets, and secondhand stores, be on the lookout for things that will create interest, warmth, and a pleasure to the senses in your classroom.

To cultivate dreams and a sense of wonder in children, surround them with soothing images and the sensory pleasures of nature.

Look for:

- straw mats
- throw rugs
- pillows, cushions, and bean bag chairs
- fabric of diverse textures, colors, thickness, and patterns from various cultures
- art prints and postcards
- nature photography and posters
- sculpture, pottery, natural baskets and other forms of art
- lap quilts and soft blankets

Use  Elements of Nature

In our safety and liability conscious programs, children are kept indoors or inside fences with materials and equipment made from plastic, concrete, and metal. Less and less do they have the opportunity to experience the pleasures of nature and the sensory delights of playing with natural materials. Recent studies show that ongoing exposure to nature is vital for the health and well-being of humans.

Ideas from the Natural World

You can provide more experiences with nature for children, indoors and outdoors, in fairly simple, inexpensive ways. Set up sensory tables filled with sand and water; create science areas with natural materials for investigation; bring in plants, pets, and gardens to care for. Expand on these with some of the following ideas:

- Place large boulders or tree stumps around the room for seating or small workspaces, for indoor climbing or an obstacle course, or as dividers to define areas of the room.
- Add twigs, rocks, shells, feathers, leaves, driftwood, marble, and other natural materials to activity centers. In the block area, they become part of the building and architecture. In the dramatic play area, they become food for people and animals. On tables, children use them for counting and classifying. In the art area, they become a part of children sensory exploration, collage, and representations.
- Include a variety of plants, trees, and flowers throughout the room. Use hanging baskets to lower ceilings and add a cozy feeling. Create a reading area where children can sit under the branch of a tree. Add plants and flowers to shelves and tables where children eat. Construct a fish pond with lily pads, indoors or outdoors (you can find kits in nurseries and home stores for reasonable prices).
- Add a small bubbling fountain or waterfall to your classroom (again, look for kits in nurseries and home stores).

Keep Flexible

Space, Schedule, and Classroom Routines

A child-centered curriculum is about creating spaces for preserving childhood. It involves slowing down and paying attention to all of the possibilities for beauty, curiosity, delight, and a sense of community in your classroom.

Rich curriculum is possible **with** each routine including meals, cleanup, self-care, moving from place to place; **with** each interaction involving inquiry, shared excitement, and problem solving; **with** time on the child's side, which means long periods of time to play, focus on interests and practice skills and friendships.

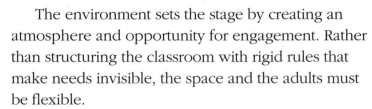

The environment sets the stage by creating an atmosphere and opportunity for engagement. Rather than structuring the classroom with rigid rules that make needs invisible, the space and the adults must be flexible.

To work as a guardian of childhood, you must be an improvisational artist, responding to needs, rearranging space, and creating new ways for discovery and relationships.

Daily schedules and routines create the ebb and flow of childhood. Too often our days with children are focused on getting them ready—to eat, go outside, take a nap, hear a story, go to school. With this mind-set, we miss the moment of *now* in childhood and the chance to meet real needs and interests. In a child-centered framework, curriculum is everything that happens.

To sum up what we mean, we've compiled the following list.

Elements of a Child-Centered Curriculum

- Large amount of time available each day for continuous self-initiated play

- Minimal number of adult agendas interrupting children's play

- Flexibility in space arrangements and schedules to respond to children's involved play

- Flexible requirements about cleaning up before continuing one's involved play in another area

- Child-initiated play themes incorporated into cleanup and group time routines

- Little distinction between transitions and play

- Turn-taking negotiated by children with teachers coaching, rather than intervening with rigid time limits

- Invented rituals to deal with difficult transitions and times when things don't feel good, as well as milestones and celebrations.

Six Basic Guidelines for

Transforming Your Teaching

to a Child-Centered Approach

As you move toward a curriculum that better reflects children's lives, use the following guidelines. These six steps will provide a more meaningful and rich experience for you and the children in your care. They will also create a stronger foundation for school readiness.

Step One: Set the stage and allow time.

Plan the environment as your basic curriculum, organizing the space and materials in an accessible, attractive, inviting way, suggesting all sorts of choices and possibilities. Allow at least one-hour blocks of time for children to engage in open-ended free choice time uninterrupted by adult ideas, agendas, and schedule demands.

Step Two: Open the space. Let children combine different areas.

Avoid being too rigid with rules that require props to stay in certain areas. For example, if dress-up clothes cannot go out of the house area, how can children become outfitted cooks at the playdough table or suited firefighters in the block area? Markers and pens may be needed for making signs in the block or dress-up areas, along with books for reading to doll babies or consulting in the design of building construction. Stock your room with an ample supply of open-ended materials (loose parts) that beg to be transported and transformed.

Step Three: Avoid interrupting significant play.

Your goal is to enable children to become truly absorbed in activities of their own choosing. As children move through the stages of play, they are able to sustain complex, cooperative play and language for longer and longer periods of time. Interrupting them with adult agendas defeats your goal of extending their attention span and independence.

Step Four: Keep the cleanup options open.

A well-meaning teacher, concerned that children learn to responsibly care for the room, often asks a child to stop and put away abandoned toys when the child is still in the middle of playing out a script. A firefighter responding to a 911 call wants to play out the story, not stop for a few minutes to pick up some discarded dress-up clothes. Quietly tidy up an area yourself, or observe when the play episode has reached a natural conclusion before requesting the children to clean up. Practice most of your cleanup requirements at cleanup time, rather than during play time.

Step Five: Refer children to each other.

Build a learning community. Young children need to see themselves as competent and resourceful. When you notice a child in need of assistance, point out another child who might be able to help. Model, support, and coach these interactions so that children develop the disposition and skills to use each other as resources. Treat conflict resolution in a similar manner. Provide routines, materials, and activities that require more than one person to make them work.

Step Six: Observe consciously.

Literally think twice before intervening!

Loose Parts

Provide open-ended materials that offer opportunities for transporting, transforming and using one's experience and imagination.

Large corporations create most children's toys and materials, which often serve as commercials for TV programs. They come with a theme and script, or a particular way to use them. How do these toys provide for children's investigation, imagination, or creativity? In most cases, they rarely do.

Loose parts is a term coined by architect Simon Nicholson, to refer to open-ended materials that provide opportunities for transporting, transforming, and using one's experience and imagination. Given the chance, children will use loose parts as invented props to support their play and investigation of the world. Children transport and transform them in remarkable ways.

To add loose parts to your environment, look for interesting, open-ended materials. Yard sales and thrift stores, as well as your own forgotten boxes at home or in storage lockers, are great sources for these kinds of materials. Here are some of our favorite ideas for these curriculum treasures.

Kitchen Curriculum

Doesn't every parent have a story of children preferring to play with pots, pans, and plastic tubs rather than a fancy new toy? Loose parts from the kitchen make great props for children's creative play. The most interesting gadgets are those with moveable parts or small compartments such as sifters, tongs, jar openers, nut crackers, egg holders, beaters and timers, ice cube trays, meat or cheese grinders, garlic presses, melon ball scoopers, and vegetable steamers. Introduce these at circle time and again at choice time.

Rope, String and Twine Curriculum

Assemble a box of rope, fabric belts, twine, string, yarn, shoelaces, and miscellaneous lengths of rope-like materials. Provide these to children, indoors or outdoors, as is, or with clothespins, pulleys, or clips.

Watch the children come up with a multitude of uses, from exploring lengths and measuring, to learning to tie, to transporting objects. (Provide for safety guidelines when first introducing the use of ropes).

Farm Curriculum

Bales of hay are inexpensive loose parts to use outdoors (and indoors for courageous teachers!). When the bale is intact, children can use it for climbing, jumping and elevating themselves. As it falls apart, hay becomes a soft place for jumping in and hiding.

Loose hay becomes a prop for dramatic play. Children can load, carry, build, and feed animals. Special caution: check for allergies before using this curriculum.

Cardboard Box Curriculum

Boxes are places to hide treasures, explore spatial relationships (how do I fit in here?), and find privacy, alone or with a friend. Boxes spark dramatic play and provide opportunities to transport objects from one place to another. Small boxes on tables offer a way to practice sorting and classifying.

Boxes are a free, never-ending source of rich curriculum for children. Get some today!

Fabric Curriculum

A collection of fabric in a variety of textures, shapes and sizes is a great addition to a child-centered curriculum. Children use fabric for sensory exploration (wrapping up, seeing through), dramatic play (costumes, blankets), and construction (making tents and hiding places). They also explore spatial concepts by covering tables, blocks, themselves, and each other with fabric. Introduce fabrics in a variety of colors and diverse cultural designs as well as ones that are sheer, sequined, shiny, rough, thick, bumpy, lacy, and velvety.

Junk Shop Curriculum

Junk shops have many interesting gadgets for play props. (Check out your own junk storage areas too!) Sometimes you don't even know why the gadget was invented. The best ones come apart and fit together or open and close. Here are some ideas: doorknobs, switches, clamps, PVC pipes, large nuts, bolts, hinges, pulleys, paint rollers, elastic cords, wrenches, hand tools, and old appliances to take apart. (Caution: check for sharp edges; cut cords and plugs off of electrical appliances.)

Food Packaging and Odd Items Curriculum

Keep a shopping bag handy in your kitchen to collect clean food packaging, small boxes, paper towel rolls and twists. Ask families to keep your classroom supplied, as well. Seek out recycling and salvage businesses, which have items for exploration and invention such as all sizes and shapes of sponges and Styrofoam; paper bags and containers; rugs; wood; plastic and tile pieces; aluminum pans; wooden and plastic spools; old telephone wire; microchip boards and keyboards; and tape of all kinds, sizes, colors and widths.

Reflecting Children's Lives

A child-centered curriculum reflects an understanding of the sensory, physical, and exploratory needs of children. In the preceding pages, you considered how to address these with your environment, materials, and activities.

Providing for children's social and emotional development is an equally important aspect of planning curriculum that reflects children's lives.

Real self-esteem is developed by focusing on children's identity, family life, and need for power and independence throughout the curriculum. Comfort with those different from oneself comes from meaningful opportunities to interact with others.

With these ideas in mind, take another look at your learning environment.

- ☐ In what ways does it let children know that they belong?
- ☐ How are their lives and interests represented and celebrated?
- ☐ What opportunities are available for children to see and explore who they are within the context of their family life, culture, and the image of a larger community?
- ☐ How do they learn empathy, not to fear, attack or form biases against others different from themselves?
- ☐ Where are the places for physical power and adventure that diminish a need to imitate media super-heroes and violent characters?

If you discovered you want to make some improvements in this area, consider the following curriculum strategies.

Me and My Family

When children see their lives and interests reflected around them, they feel safe, known, and affirmed. Expand these representations of the children's lives with the school year.

- Create ongoing classroom displays and photo albums that include children's lives, past and present, at home and in preschool.
- Regularly include food and positive mealtime experiences that are familiar to the children; this includes inviting parents to do classroom cooking projects as part of the curriculum.
- Make "show and share" a daily part of your program. Rather than having one day for showing off commercial toys from home, add items with special meaning from home to your activity centers. Introduce these items with guidelines for use.
- Add books, pictures, and dramatic play props that reflect current family events and interests (for example, birth of a new baby, moving, parent's job, and family celebrations).
- Make puzzles, matching games, and paper dolls for dramatic play using photos of the children, their families, and their homes and neighborhood. Enlarge the photos at a copy center, mount and cut them out of heavy cardboard or foamcore.
- Add a new activity area to your room: the Classroom and Community News Center. This can replace traditional "show and tell" routines with photos, stories, and children's work, as well as handmade books, family albums, and other objects from home. Include a camera, pens, paper, and

ready-made blank books for children to participate in documenting the history of your time together in the classroom.

Learning About Others

Children are naturally curious about other people. With classification as a primary developmental theme, they are busy noticing similarities and differences. Provide opportunities for this with images that show differences.

- Display pictures depicting the ways people carry objects: babies, water, and food. Add props such as baskets, backpacks, buckets, bamboo poles, and fabric slings for the children to role play.
- Read books and post pictures reflecting the kinds of shelters people live in. Include rocks, twigs, marble pieces, bales of straw, plaster of Paris, leaves, and bamboo that can be used for construction activities.
- Bake different varieties of bread found across cultures such as pocket bread, fry bread, yeasted bread, unleavened bread, hum bao, injera, bagels, and croissants.
- Explore the ways families live together through photos of families in your program and children's books depicting all kinds of families.
- Include different family compositions, cultures, celebrations, traditions, and housing arrangements.

Countering Bias

Counter stereotypes by showing contemporary life and typical ways of living, rather than exotic activities or uncommon celebrations. Other ways to counter fear of difference and the development of bias include the following:

Create places

for physical

power

and adventure

in your

programs,

inside and

outside.

Reclaim

childhood

from commercial

interests.

- Create positive sensory experiences with various shades of brown and black (paint, clay, and playdough with extracts of vanilla, peppermint, licorice, and almond).
- Watch your language to ensure you don't perpetuate unintended stereotypes such as only men are firefighters, doctors, or powerful people; only women are gentle and able to nurture; only people of color have culture; children always live with their parents; everyone celebrates Christian holidays; and all families have enough money for birthday parties.
- Respond positively to children who point out differences that they notice; help them feel that differences are normal, interesting, and welcome.
- Display photos of the children in your group embedded in a mural of children from all races, all economic conditions, and wearing all kinds of clothes.

Places for Physical Development Themes

A central developmental theme for preschoolers revolves around their bodies: how to live with their vulnerability and sense of powerlessness; and what to do with their ever-growing limbs and energy.

Ripe with imaginations, children naturally seek out representations of physical power and adventure to claim as their own.

Too often we trivialize children's needs for self-esteem and identity affirmation. We make comments such as, "What a big boy!," "Nice job!," and "That's so cute!" At the same time, we encourage children to suppress or negate their bodies and energy. We downplay—and thus hand over to TV, movies, video games, and commercial toys—children's need for adventure, risk-taking, and boldness.

To provide for this extremely physical time of life, develop obstacle courses, changing them often to add ever-increasing challenges. When you let children use real tools, do meaningful work, and take acceptable risks, you help them to feel competent and powerful.

To counter children's fascination with commercialized superheroes, regularly include representations of strong and powerful people who are not gender-stereotyped. Retell classroom activities as an adventure story with the children as characters; create plots that reflect the tension of their developmental concerns: good and evil, strong and weak, acceptable and unacceptable.

Collaborate

for Another Look at Your Environment and Daily Schedule

After working to incorporate the ideas of this chapter, ask a co-worker to help you re-assess your environment. Encourage her or him to use the checklist on pages 36-38 and walk around the different areas of your room, writing responses. Under "Already present," have your co-worker list those items observed. Then meet together to brainstorm the items to add or eliminate under the "Goal" sections.

Sometimes another person's perspective will clarify areas you have mastered or want to work on further. Collaboration enhances learning opportunities for you and your colleagues.

Assess Your Environment
and Daily Schedule

Arrangement of Environment

- Materials are visible, accessible, aesthetically organized, and inviting.
  ☐ Already present: ☐ Goal:

- Loose parts (open-ended materials) readily available inside and outside.
  ☐ Already present: ☐ Goal:

- Diverse elements of texture, shape, and the natural world to invite exploration and discovery.
  ☐ Already present: ☐ Goal:

- Opportunities for transporting, combining, and transforming materials.
  ☐ Already present: ☐ Goal:

- Visual images representing a range of roles and cultural expressions to cultivate comfort with differences.
  ☐ Already present: ☐ Goal:

- Representations of children's lives and interests around the room (photos, sketches, objects with stories).
  ☐ Already present: ☐ Goal:

- Flexibility of space, allowing for expansion when many children are working in the same area.
  ☐ Already present: ☐ Goal:

- Minimal restrictions to moving in and out of areas.
  ☐ Already present: ☐ Goal:

- Places for physical activity and power.
  ☐ Already present: ☐ Goal:

- Opportunities for adventure and risk taking.
  ☐ Already present: ☐ Goal:

Daily Routines

- Large amount of time each day for continuous self-initiated play.
  ☐ Already present: ☐ Goal:

- Minimal number of adult agendas interrupting children's play.
  ☐ Already present: ☐ Goal:

- Flexibility in space and schedule to respond to children's interest.
  ☐ Already present: ☐ Goal:

- Cleanup not always required before a child moves to another area.
  ☐ Already present: ☐ Goal:

- Play themes incorporated into cleanup and group-time routines.
  ☐ Already present: ☐ Goal:

- Little distinction between transitions and play.
  ☐ Already present: ☐ Goal:

- Taking turns negotiated by children with coaching from teachers (rather than teachers setting rigid time limits).
  ☐ Already present: ☐ Goal:

About Your

Current

Environment

*Looking over
the goals
you identified
with
your co-worker,
begin to
make plans
to achieve them.*

What are your priorities? List them as next steps for yourself.

Where can you get the resources and support you need (for example, co-workers, parents, community)?

Our Dream Became
Our Curriculum: A Story of an

Outdoor Play Space

Laurie S. Cornelius,
ECFE Lab School Director

A few years ago, our new child care center, a lab school for Clark College Early Childhood Education students in Vancouver, Washington, was faced with a playground that was terribly inadequate and needed to be replaced. Basically, it was an empty play space with a few old and decaying structures that weren't safe. As these structures were torn down, my role as the director became funding and creating a new outdoor play space. It became a journey that was an emergent curriculum project for both adults and children. And it left us believing that we should never settle for less than our dreams.

Drawing on our own childhood memories

To develop our thinking about the kind of outdoor space we wanted to create, I decided to have parents and staff meet together to think about the play memories we had as children, and experiences we thought were valuable enough to ensure for children. The group generated a huge list with many overlapping memories of playing outdoors. Play themes included risk-taking, feeling powerful, constructing, hauling, transporting, digging, moving things to and from, having privacy, and unstructured playing time with friends. We remembered different sounds and textures, seasonal changes, smells, and prickly, sandy, and muddy things. A source of water always meant endless possibilities for play.

This story will inspire and encourage you in your efforts to enrich your environment.

As we looked at this list, we asked ourselves what elements were involved in each of these experiences. In other words, if you liked to go and hide, then you need places in your environment to do that; if you liked to build dams or forts, then you need water and rocks and logs to build with; if you liked to lie under a tree, then you need shade trees. Some of our memories were of being raised on farms, jumping from bales and playing in the hay. We added to our list all the props and processes that would have to be built into an environment to provide for these childhood experiences.

As I started working with Candy Bennett, a grant writer, she mentioned that there was federal block grant money designated for parks and asked if that was closer to the model we were after. We got involved in brainstorming to develop a concept that might be fundable by a broad spectrum of our community, including block grant monies. Our concept was that with upwards of 60 percent of children in child care, children aren't spending significant time in parks any more. Instead, their time outdoors is spent in fenced-in playgrounds with few of the opportunities that a good park has to offer.

There was a significant shift in our thinking as we started to look at child care and early childhood outdoor environments as parks. This moved us away from the school recess concept with the limited view that all you need is gross motor play to run and get your wiggles out so you will be better behaved inside. Returning again to our big list of childhood memories, we asked ourselves how we could use these elements to create a park concept inside a playground fence. As our thinking began to transform, so did our approach to fundraising.

We knew that if we were to sell this concept to funders, we would have to get a buy-in that reflected deeper understandings than the usual idea of a climbing structure as a play space. I went through the phone book and found an architect, Ron Matela, available to not only walk through our empty outdoor play area with us, but also willing to spend innumerable hours talking about our philosophy, the value of outdoor space, and the experiences of childhood.

Building on the value of risk-taking
One of our greatest challenges was to provide for risk-taking while still keeping kids safe in our program. We wrestled with how to translate

everybody's childhood memory of spending hours and hours outside, alone and with friends, exploring and having adventures with no adults around. All of our memories included taking risks that we knew wouldn't win adult approval. These risks often took on an air of mischief and misbehaving, but no one experienced any significant harm from them.

I strongly believe that taking risks is part of childhood, especially within the security of a family setting or child care program. If you don't get to take risks as a child, you aren't likely to have good judgment about risk-taking as an adult. Our center's evolving discussions about this strengthened our philosophy to create a play space that would allow children to take risks and avoid letting our adult fears impede this. My sense is that often an adult watches an exploring or adventuresome child and gets fearful. This quickly translates into the adult either stopping the child in the name of protection or passing along that fear to the child.

Our discussions on providing for risk-taking in the new play space design were intense, illuminating, and growthful for us all. We decided that we would need to keep our fear away from the children. We would allow ourselves to move into physical proximity where safety might be a strong concern. We would try to first use descriptive language with a child before intervening to stop something that had some particular risk involved. Our hope was that if we allowed a four-year-old child to fall when he rides his trike too fast around a curve, he won't have to experiment with this in a car when he's sixteen. We asked ourselves, "If a child tries to jump over a log and skins her knee, is that more dangerous than never understanding her body's capability as she grows and takes on more physical challenges?" I worry about a growing person's ability to self-impose needed limits if these limits have always been externally imposed by someone else.

What happens if our group care settings don't allow children the freedom to take risks and to feel capable of doing difficult things? How do they learn to make good judgments about whether something is safe if they have never experienced the consequences of their limitations? We have to allow children to experience little physical hurts so that they can learn natural consequences. In doing this, they start to develop a sense of their capabilities. They also have an experience of celebrating their success in trying something over and over again and finally learning to do it. These developmental understandings evolved out of our numerous adult discussions of our childhood memories. We decided we wanted the challenge of that emotional element to be in our planning design along with the physical challenges. The two go hand in hand.

Adapting what we know works indoors

Another significant factor in the evolution of our outdoor planning was to learn from how we arranged the inside environment, something we're pretty good at. Rather than having one big space to run around in, we decided to think in terms of learning centers and to create different outdoor areas for certain experiences. We had our list of childhood memories to help us define the kind of areas we wanted.

Indoors we typically use cupboards and shelving units to divide up space and create smaller group interest areas. How might we do that outdoors using materials more indigenous to the natural world? To plan for some of the elements we had been discussing, we began planting trees, bushes, and hedges and adding rocks, logs, and stumps to naturally divide the space along these lines. We created a garden area, a quiet area, and several hill climbing and rolling areas. We created places to hide, dig in the sand, build structures, ride trikes, and make up dramas and games with friends. We considered the diverse sounds and textures of our childhoods in the out of doors—trees rustling, water gurgling, rocks crashing and splashing in a lake, tires thumping over wooden slats, branches, and leaves and prickly things brushing against our skin. Was there a way to provide for these as we divided up the space?

We knew it was our responsibility to supervise children at all times, but we wanted to create spaces where kids had a sense of privacy and space away from adults—while still being visible to us. We started looking at how we could clump plantings of trees and bushes, create pits and hills so that the landscape would shape this feeling, and provide a variety of clusters of smaller options for children's play. The decision about the few pieces of commercial equipment we purchased were based on how the equipment provided for social interaction and individualized creativity, along with large motor skills.

Returning again and again to our philosophy

Perhaps the experience with our little covered bridge has taught us the most about putting our philosophy into practice. We originally designed the bridge as a place for children to ride their trikes across to hear a different kind of sound than on the cement. This idea came from our initial brainstorming session, and we thought it would be neat to make this part of the bike path that runs all around the play space. Then the children discovered new ways to use the bridge. Some of them began climbing over the railing to practice jumping over the rocks below. Adults nearly had heart attacks and wanted to quickly make rules so this couldn't happen.

This led to a discussion which resulted in the decision that no rules could be made quickly without really observing what the children are doing. Our observations will determine whether a rule we're inclined to make might be blocking some children's capabilities. If we make a general rule because a child may get hurt, what are we doing to all the children who can do this without the likelihood of getting hurt?

We finally asked ourselves, "Are the children who are trying to do this able to do it?" That was the best question that ever evolved because it forced us to look more closely at who was really taking this risk. The children that weren't really competent at it yet were climbing over the railing, but they were hesitantly watching, not jumping. There were other kids who weren't even climbing over the railing, but just watching from the sidelines. When we observed, we saw children at all of these stages. A rule suitable for one of them, would limit the development of others.

That was the first big discussion that challenged our philosophy. Very shortly after that we had a group of very competent five year olds who had been in gymnastics. They decided to climb up into the rafters of the bridge and hang upside down. So there they were, dangling upside down as children on trikes approached the bridge, heading toward them. More heart attacks. This didn't seem like a good idea. We were really worried. When we asked ourselves if the children were competent to do this, the answer was yes. When we asked if it was safe, the answer was no. We decided we needed a guideline.

We came up with the guideline that the children must find a partner who would close the bridge. Together they would figure out how to close it, and then the upside down hanging would be safe enough. With guidelines rather than rules, we discovered a whole new level of possibilities for children to become problem solvers.

Using portable props for play themes

Another set of elements from our childhood memories involved construction and moveable props. We knew we had to have stuff to carry around and to do so on a variety of surfaces—grass, sand, concrete. Gradually we have collected big pieces of driftwood to add as props. You'll see kids drag them around and often call to others to help with a heavy one. "We can't move this. Help us." It's so exciting to see. They have a plan and it goes some place. One day it will be on the grass and another day in the sand pit.

I believe that by far the most important play props we have in the space are the rocks. We never would have considered that, but we knew from our memories that big rocks were important in building dams, building forts and pretend camp fires, and blocking off streets for games. Because it was a universal in our memories of childhood we decided on big rocks for hauling and building — rocks too big to throw, but heavy enough to make hauling a worthwhile effort. The rocks move everywhere in our play space, with the exception of keeping them off of the climber where they could cause harm if dropped.

Another reason for including big rocks is because children feel powerful when they move big heavy things and this is a key element of our philosophy. For other opportunities to feel powerful we also created three tiers of hills so that children could get higher than the adults below. They get a sense of power from being able to scan the environment from above. Also, by simply planting bushes of different sizes and shapes, we made it possible for children to play hide and seek, peek-a-boo, or run-around-tag for hours. Tucking some of these bushes up closer to the fence, we've created a feeling of privacy, taking care to prune in some windows for visibility for the adults. This sense of independence is another component to helping children feel powerful.

Today our concept of needing ongoing planning of the outdoor space has evolved into funding a specific teacher for the job. She has her own storage space with supplies and she plans curriculum for the outdoors in a way that parallels what teachers do indoors—putting out new props for the children to discover and respond to, keeping an eye on the evolving play, and planning for emerging developmental interests and skills. When teachers and children come out into the space she gives guidance to the adults about effective ways to supervise and work with guidelines. She's like a lead teacher for the out-of-doors and classroom teachers team with her when they have ideas they want to bring outside. Getting this staff position would never have happened if we hadn't opened up our thinking and let our dreams become our curriculum.

This story is about creating visions, for children and for adults. Boredom, fear, and hopelessness can eat us alive. We have to find ways of breaking loose from a sense of powerlessness, the feeling that things have changed and there's nothing we can do about it. I think we get caught in the reality of today and develop short-term solutions for things, forgetting to think about the long-term implications. Do the decisions we make for children in our programs today support the values we have for their childhood? Are our decisions developing capable people, or are they suppressing competency in order to make life easier or more convenient for adults?

The resources that emerged for our play space came about as a result of a vision that people believed in. Their vision was more than support for a project. The project was a concrete representation of a vision. The vision is the dream that we nurtured in each head; people translated that vision into specific action.

Putting the *Child* back in DAP

3

Is it childhood

or school

that guides

your thinking

when planning

curriculum?

When you hear the term developmentally appropriate practice, what comes to mind? Do you think of school readiness activities and lesson plans watered down to work better for younger children? **Or** is your image one of children spending long periods of time engrossed in building elaborate structures with blocks? **Is** it childhood or school that guides your thinking in planning curriculum?

Teacher's Ideas versus

Child's Interest

Keeping the

definition

of DAP

in mind,

read through

Ron's and Lena's

curriculum plans

below. Which

do you think

represents

developmentally

appropriate

practice?

In recent years, many early childhood professionals have come to think of developmentally appropriate practice (DAP) as a curriculum. However, DAP is not a curriculum in and of itself. Rather, it is a practice that involves responding and planning for individual children's development within a cultural context.

Ron's Color Curriculum

Ron is planning curriculum activities to teach children their colors. He's been looking through activity books for ideas he thinks the children will like. For each week in September, Ron will teach a color of the week. Here are some of the activities he's planned for each color.

- Mix the color of the week for painting at the easel.
- Have a collage art project with different shapes of that color to glue.
- Label the colors in a bulletin board display.
- Play "Can you find something of this color?"
- Put selected pieces from the color lotto game out on the table.
- Dismiss the children by the colors they are wearing.

Lena's Color Curriculum

All week, four-year-old Lena has been pouring and stirring paint in the containers at the art table. Corrine, her teacher, sees this interest and arranges for her to discover something new today. Corrine sets out only red and blue paint. Going to the easel, Lena takes a brush and makes a few strokes of red on her paper. Next she uses the blue to paint a few letters in her name. Putting the brush again in the red paint and sweeping it across the paper she exclaims,, Look, it's changing!"

Corrine responds with a smile, "You mix it, it changes." Lena begins pouring the red paint into the blue, stirring it with her brush. She calls out her understanding. "Corrine, it changes to red-blue." The moment of new understanding is visible on her face and in her voice as Lena bursts out with, "Look, Corrine, now it's changing to purple!"

Observation

is the heart of the matter

Observation is at the heart of child-centered, emergent curriculum planning. Observing children will teach you a great deal about child development. It will help you identify additional skills you might want to learn. You will become resourceful, imaginative, and more curious about children. You will remember why you love this work.

When you compare Ron's and Lena's color curriculums, you discover the foundation of DAP—planning from close observation and careful analysis of children rather than centering on lessons from activity books. The name of each curriculum reflects a clear difference. The thinking of Ron, the teacher, is the focus of the first curriculum. The interests of Lena, the child, is the center of the second.

The following table contrasts and compares these two curriculums.

Ron's Color Curriculum	Lena's Color Curriculum
Ideas for curriculum come from books and what the teacher wants the children to learn.	Observation of children's interests and activities are the basis for curriculum ideas.
The focus is on exposing children to different colors and learning color names.	The focus is on planning for discovery and exploration that will lead to deeper interests and understandings of how colors are created.
The curriculum direction and desired outcomes are predetermined by the teacher. Children do teacher-planned projects with little understanding or even interest in why.	Curriculum direction is set by the children. The desired outcomes are focused on children learning to take initiative to pursue things they want to understand.
The curriculum covers the names and recognition of four colors.	The curriculum gets "uncovered" as a child's interest in mixing colors is discovered and sustained, with teacher planning that builds in possibilities for the child to acquire deeper understandings.

Skills Required for a

Child-Centered

Curriculum

Learning to be an observer, gathering data about who the children are, their interests, questions, strengths, and challenges is the starting point for building a child-centered curriculum. Observation is a critical tool for ongoing assessment, planning, and response to children.

The most difficult aspect of observing is to see with objectivity. When observing, adults tend to quickly interpret situations and come to conclusions before gathering data and analyzing it objectively.

Our backgrounds, life experiences, values, and expectations all influence how we filter observations and information. To observe more objectively, we must practice suspending our filters and initial interpretations of what we are seeing.

Practice Learning to Observe

To practice noting the difference between descriptive observations and interpretations, find a magazine photograph of children and adults involved in some kind of activity.

Quickly write a list of statements about what you see in the photograph. Read through your list. Put a "D" next to the words and statements that are specific descriptions of what is in the picture. These are usually the elements of a situation that most people would identify and agree upon.

> Observing children is both an art and a skill. Observation skills involve an objective, detailed collection of data and an eye for the meaning and richness of each child's developmental experience.

Now look for statements that are interpretations of the scene, rather than more objective descriptions. Put an "I" next to these. These are conclusions based on your own filters or subconscious cues picked up from the scene. For more practice, look at the chart below and note the difference.

Descriptive Data: The Skill of Observation	Interpretations: The Art of Observing
One adult, one child, and one baby	A family: a mom with her two children
The adult is holding the baby on her lap, looking down at the child, smiling.	The mom thinks her baby is so cute.
The child is standing behind the adult with her hands covering the adult's eyes.	The child is jealous because the mom is paying too much attention to the baby.

Under the "Descriptive Data" column, only observable facts are noted. This data is important to distinguish from assumptions you might be making. The data in the "Interpretations" column should be based on observable facts, not assumptions. As you look at the chart again, notice how the observer could be jumping to conclusions without adequate data for her interpretations.

The following questions can guide you in developing the art of observation.

Questions for Analyzing Observation Notes

- What led me to make these statements?
- Are there subtle cues (for example, body posture, facial expressions, clothing, or colors that influenced my thinking?
- Are my statements based on any filters from my own experience, background, or values?

Your interpretations are not necessarily wrong, nor do you want to ignore them. In fact, interpretation is the art of observation. Interpreting descriptive data and underlying cues becomes the foundation of child-centered planning.

The goal is to be as objective as possible. You want to be aware of your filters and biases and how they influence the way you informally collect data (information) about children. Each response and plan you make should be based on what you understand about the child and your own values and goals for the situation.

Questions to Guide Interpretation and Planning

- What did you specifically see?
- How would you name the essence of this experience for this child?
- What does this child know how to do?
- What does this child find frustrating?
- How does this child feel about herself or himself?

Ask yourself repeatedly, "What did I specifically see?" Formulating objective descriptions is a critical skill in the observation process. Write your descriptions down and when you notice you have made an overly general statement, ask yourself,

"What did I specifically see that makes me say that?" Find ways to back up your statements with descriptive data.

For example, if you observed, "The child was angry," try to answer, "What did I specifically see that made me think he was angry?" Specific descriptions related to anger might be, "I saw the child frown, stomp his feet, and yell."

Initially, try to avoid drawing any conclusions so you can practice the skill of objectively gathering clues and information before making interpretations and plans.

As you move to the art of interpretation, put yourself in the children's shoes and consider what you have just seen through their eyes.

To understand the children's point of view, consider the following:

- What are they trying to do in their play?
- What experiences, knowledge, and skill are they building on?
- What questions, inventions, or problems are they encountering?
- What do they find meaningful? Frustrating? Challenging?
- What might they want from you or their playmates?

Observation and Recording Skills

To enhance your skill as an observer in collecting data, use the following guidelines.

Objectivity. To record objectively is to avoid making initial judgments or broad generalizations. Objective recording strives to be non-interpretive. Saying, "The boys were much too noisy and out of control," interprets the meaning of a behavior that isn't specifically described. In contrast, "During cleanup Jonathan and Jason yelled across the room at each other, arguing as to who was the last to play with the blocks," describes the behavior labeled as "too noisy and out of control." This objectivity allows you to assess the context and any personal filters that might be influencing your interpretation.

Specificity. Record specific details regarding the number of children and adults involved in an activity, the amount and kind of materials available, the passage of time, and so forth. This provides detail as to the context.

Directness. Recording direct quotes is a difficult skill to master, but it is very useful when analyzing observation notes. For instance, a note that includes the sentence, "Jason said, 'I was playing with that first,'" indicates that the child has language skills for resolving conflicts.

Completeness. Completeness in recording involves describing incidents from beginning to end. A complete recording describes the setting, who was involved, what action occurred, what the reaction was, and how the incident occurred.

Inclusion of Mood Clues. Mood clues are tones of voice, facial expressions, body posture, hand gestures, and other non-verbal body clues. Including mood clues in recording observations helps you make inferences about the social and emotional climate of a situation.

Practice Interpreting Observations

Read the following observation description.

Derek is standing at the sand table, playing with large plastic dinosaurs. He digs in the sand, burying one of the plastic dinosaurs and a dinosaur skeleton. "This one has been dead a long time," he says, pointing to the skeleton dinosaur. "This one isn't dead yet," he says smiling, "I better not bury it."

Derek grabs a tiny shovel and pickax and begins uncovering each of the dinosaurs he buried. Is he exploring something about death? He seems to understand that bones are what is left after one dies.

He digs up the large plastic dinosaur and starts putting sand down its big open mouth. "Here, you better eat your vegetables. I'm going to fill you all up with vegetables," he says, filling the dinosaur with sand. "I need a funnel to fill him up." He probably thinks that it will take less time to fill up the dinosaur with a funnel. Derek is a very smart child. His play is sophisticated.

To practice your observation skills, write down each sentence from the above description under one of the two columns on the next page.

Descriptions

_____
_____
_____
_____
_____
_____
_____
_____
_____
_____
_____
_____
_____
_____
_____
_____
_____
_____
_____
_____
_____
_____
_____
_____
_____
_____
_____
_____

Interpretations

_____
_____
_____
_____
_____
_____
_____
_____
_____
_____
_____
_____
_____
_____
_____
_____
_____
_____
_____
_____
_____
_____
_____
_____
_____
_____
_____

Next, ask yourself these questions:

What does Derek know how to do? Be specific.

What does he find frustrating? Add any specific indicators.

How does he feel about himself? What clues tell you this?

What is the essence of this experience for Derek? Name its meaning or theme in a phrase.

A Closer Look

The observer of Derek used many descriptive statements, including direct quotes of what he said. With these direct statements, she had data that led her to interpret that Derek understood some aspects of death and is exploring more. She had less than adequate information here to support the interpretations of the last two sentences.

Perhaps her assessment that Derek is smart and a sophisticated player is built on an accumulation of observations. If so, she could strengthen the validity of these interpretative statements by making reference to how this observation is consistent with others in the past.

Because observation takes practice, on page XX you'll find a blank form to copy and use. Spending 15 to 30 minutes observing a child or small group of children will give you data to interpret and then use for curriculum planning. Start by filling out the left side of the page, noting things you specifically observe. At the end of your observation period, read this column over and fill in the Interpretations column as you again ask yourself the following questions:

☐ What are they trying to do in their play?

☐ What experiences, knowledge, and skill are they building on?

☐ What questions, inventions, or problems are they encountering?

☐ What do they find meaningful? Frustrating? Challenging?

☐ What might they want from you or their playmates?

Program Observations

Observation Setting: _____

Time and Date of Observation: _____

Observer:_____

Descriptions

_____

_____

_____

_____

_____

_____

_____

_____

_____

_____

_____

_____

_____

_____

_____

_____

_____

_____

Interpretations

_____

_____

_____

_____

_____

_____

_____

_____

_____

_____

_____

_____

_____

_____

_____

_____

_____

_____

Developing an Eye for

Significant Play in Your Program

Another way to practice your observation skills for appropriate curriculum practice is to look for key elements of children's play. These will alert you to their developmental process. When children are involved in good, complex play, you will see them doing the following. (If these elements are missing, you can develop goals for yourself to provide them.)

Are the children…

☐ making props for their own play?
observations:

☐ engaging peers and/or adults in dramatic play?
observations:

☐ transforming space and material to meet their needs?
observations:

☐ negotiating roles and problems with their peers?
observations:

☐ continuing thematic play from day to day?
observations:

☐ using special vocabulary with increasingly complex sentence structure?
observations:

Notes

About Your Current Observation Practices

Use this page to reflect on your current observation practices.

How would you assess your current skills?

How often do you observe children?

What are the barriers that keep you from regular observation?

What strategies could you use to overcome these barriers?

A Curriculum of Discovery

For the Children, and for Me

Journal Entries from Esther Swenson,
Preschool Teacher

As part of a class with Margie Carter and Deb Curtis on developmentally appropriate curriculum, I began to see myself as a researcher. Margie and Deb had encouraged our class to consistently provide a set of open-ended materials for the children and to collect observations of their interactions with these materials and each other over a period of time.

At first I and other class members just paid attention to what the children did with the material and what they found fun and pleasurable. Then we began observing what the children invented and understood through their self-directed activities and what they talked about, represented, and connected to their previous experiences.

> Read this story to see how observing changed one teacher's approach to curriculum.

This research data became the basis for us to ask ourselves, "What other materials might extend their experiences or help them represent their ideas and feelings?" Answering this question gave me and other class members more ideas for materials to offer. Margie and Deb also encouraged all of us to think about what role the children needed us to play in the process.

By working on this assignment and closely observing the children in my class, I began to discover a new way of approaching curriculum planning. Here are some of the journal entries I kept during this process.

4/6

I began providing woodworking materials for the kids on a daily basis because I wanted to find ways to work with them on building projects. As I looked closely, however, I saw that their primary interest was in exploring the mechanisms of how the tools worked.

At first the children just seemed interested in the individual materials. They explored the different shapes of the wood pieces, experimented with the moving parts of the tools, pounded with the hammer, and so on. Then they began to see how things worked together. Some stacked the wood pieces, others tried pounding nails into the wood. Still another pounded the wood scraps with the hammer to break and splinter the wood.

4/9

The kids were really attentive and remembered the work that they had done the day before. Sometimes they continued with their previous work and sometimes they took the wood, nails, and screws off to begin something new. In either case, they always used a wood base. They seem so pleased to be working on an ongoing project, adding more changes each day.

4/12

I keep adding new shapes of wood and different tools. Each time I do, the children explore the aspects of the new materials before combining them with familiar ones. At one point, I offered paint and it took the children in an entirely different direction. Their attention shifted to naming what they were making.

4/22

After working on something for weeks, one child decided she had made a bird feeder. Another child liked that idea and joined in the discussion. They began describing what a bird feeder needed and explored ways to change the creation to make it "really a bird feeder."

5/2

As I look back on this project, I realize that every time the children used the tools they seemed more confident, focusing more on what they could do and less on the tools themselves. They discovered what they were capable of doing by repeating actions and activities, and then by challenging themselves with some new task. They learned how to implement their ideas.

They learned they could teach each other how to use tools, answer each other's questions, and share tools. I was amazed to watch this, as I had never thought of them as able to do this on their own.

I mostly played the role of prop manager, cheerleader, and observer. I discovered that children learn by having materials consistently available to them, and they can explore and come up with questions and answers from their own initiative. I now understand that my role is to provide the opportunities for them to do their learning.

What I've learned is that children can come up with the greatest ideas— their own discovery in the midst of play is so wonderful. It's important to watch for that and let children take the lead. Their ownership of an activity gives it great momentum, enthusiasm, and appeal.

Keeping observation notes of my discoveries helped me focus on what I was seeing and learning. In many ways this whole process has transformed my thinking about teaching—I see my role in an entirely different way. Now I come into the classroom looking to see what the children have as an agenda and how I might build on that. Rather than directing things, my role is to guide what is already happening. Everything is always in motion. One thing leads to the next, and the children are constantly engaged.

I now understand more about child development because I closely observe the children and really become part of their space, instead of having just a formal idea or theory. This understanding helps me to be more in tune with what the children are experiencing right now. I use this approach all the time. It's the best!

Redefining Curriculum Themes

Redefining theme planning—by observing children and putting their interests first—is an important part of adopting a child-centered, emergent curriculum approach.

4

Because the weather warmed up, Amanda decided to bring the sensory table outside for her group of three-year-olds. The first day, she brought a large plastic tub filled with bird seed and a variety of baskets and containers. **At once,** the children began filling and pouring the seeds into the containers and baskets. Then one child carried a full basket across the play yard, calling "Birdie, Birdie, here's your food." Soon the entire group was filling containers and spreading bird seed throughout the yard. **The next day,** Amanda filled the sensory table with water and added containers, spouts, and buckets. Again, the children initially played at the table, but before long, their activity turned to carrying the water across the yard. **Noticing** this transportation theme, Amanda brought out toy trucks, buses, and wagons. Then she added lunch boxes, baskets with handles, bags, and boxes. All week, the children's play involved loading, carrying, wheeling, pushing, and unloading things across the yard.

Most preschool curriculum is planned around themes. As if they are important lessons to be learned, themes become the focus of bulletin boards, group times, and art activities throughout the week.

Transportation is a common theme in preschool curriculum. Typically, a teacher will include art activities, finger plays, dramatic play, and field trips to help children learn about trucks, boats, trains, and planes. Teachers search curriculum recipe books for these ideas and activities, never stopping to consider what the children's interest or current understandings are about the theme.

In the previous description, Amanda came to the theme of transportation in a very different way. She used her observation skills to discover the children's theme of transportation. Redefining theme planning—by observing children and putting their interests first—is an important part of adopting a child-centered, emergent curriculum approach.

From Topical Themes to

Developmental Themes

Looking at something from a child's perspective helps you redefine the notion of themes. Given the opportunity, children will pursue tasks and skills that are optimal for their individual developmental level. As skilled observers of children, teachers can discover developmental themes for curriculum planning.

Traditional Theme Planning	Developmental Theme Planning
The teacher picks the theme and plans a variety of activities to cover the information.	The teacher observes children to uncover the developmental themes they are exploring. The teacher provides further materials and activities to sustain the interest.
The teacher designs activities to provide information and test for correct answers.	The teacher bases her or his approach on inquiry and learning, which is focused on real lives, relationships, and issues.
Teachers place emphasis on "naming to know" and reciting information she or he wants children to learn.	The teacher plans materials and activities to provoke curiosity and exploration of new ideas and questions that the children generate.
Teachers assess children's missing skills and knowledge in order to plan what to teach them.	The teacher places emphasis on "doing to know"—interaction and investigation with materials, people, and ideas interesting to the children.
The teacher bases his or her approach on a narrow, simplistic view of learning and school readiness, focusing only on basic skills.	The teacher's planning revolves around children's strengths and interests. Discovering and building on children's existing questions and ideas is central to the process.

In this chart, notice the difference between a traditional approach to theme planning and an approach that focuses on uncovering the children's themes.

Children's Play Themes

The following sections include a variety of ways to identify children's developmental themes. **Use the following play themes** to create a child-centered, emergent curriculum. **Remember to observe** for children's themes during their play and conversation and provide additional materials and activities to extend their curriculum.

Piaget identified four stages of children's play that are useful for planning and responding to children in relevant ways: exploration, construction play, pretend play, and games with rules.

When you closely observe children at play, you will see these developmental themes underlying their approach to play. The following stories offer an example of each stage of play, and show several ways to provide materials and activities to enhance each play theme.

Exploration

Frankie is playing in the housekeeping area. He stands in front of the play refrigerator opening and closing the door, over and over again. He seems to have no interest in what's on the shelves, but instead is listening intently to the squeezing sound the door makes as he closes it.

Children use their senses to try things out, find out how things work, and learn cause and effect. To help them enhance their play, ask yourselves questions like the following—and answer them from a child's perspective.

- How does this feel, sound, taste, smell, move?
- What parts and properties does this have?
- What can I make this thing do?

Provide for Exploration

Once a theme emerges in children's play, plan activities and interactions to sustain and enrich their learning. One idea is to make collections of things available to the children—a collection of loose parts is a great way to provision the environment.

Let the children explore the following collections on their own, use the collections in combination with each other, or offer them to a child to enhance the pursuit of an interest or idea. Sensory materials and loose parts like those described in chapter 2 are the best for children who are involved in exploratory play. Here are more ideas.

Tubes and Cylinders. PVC pipe; toilet paper and paper towel rolls; kaleidoscopes; clear plastic tubing of different lengths and thicknesses.

Balls. Ping Pong ball, whiffle ball, golf ball, rubber ball, Nerf ball, racquetball, baseball, beach ball, tennis ball, softball, cotton ball, teething ball, Styrofoam ball, string ball, yarn ball, pom-poms.

Letting the children put the balls, tubes, and cylinders together will prompt exploration of fitting balls in tubes, watching them roll through, and filling tubes with balls.

Things that Tickle and Jingle. Feathers, soft brushes, fur, wigs, scarves, silk, feather duster, tinsel; cow bell, jingle bell, clog bell, wrist bells, ankle bells, school bell, brass bell, wind chimes.

Things to See Through. Eyeglasses, sunglasses, goggles, binoculars, telescope, camera lens, Plexiglas, Mylar, plastic bottle, theater gel, colored cellophane, magnifying glass, microscope, jeweler's loupe.

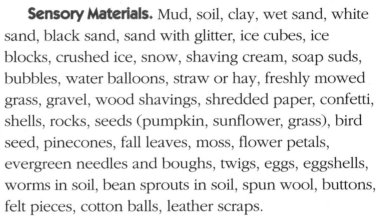

Sensory Materials. Mud, soil, clay, wet sand, white sand, black sand, sand with glitter, ice cubes, ice blocks, crushed ice, snow, shaving cream, soap suds, bubbles, water balloons, straw or hay, freshly mowed grass, gravel, wood shavings, shredded paper, confetti, shells, rocks, seeds (pumpkin, sunflower, grass), bird seed, pinecones, fall leaves, moss, flower petals, evergreen needles and boughs, twigs, eggs, eggshells, worms in soil, bean sprouts in soil, spun wool, buttons, felt pieces, cotton balls, leather scraps.

Put these materials in a tub or sensory table, alone or in combination with scoops, funnels, and tubes, and watch children become engaged in deep exploration and sensory joy!

Construction

Play

Jason carefully searches through the bucket of blocks for the long rectangle. He begins building by attaching a set of wheels to a base. He adds a set of doors and a roof. As he puts short, square pieces on the top he says, "I'm making a car."

Children seem to have a definite plan for exploration. ***Think about how a child would answer these questions.***

- How can I combine these different things?
- What can I build with these?
- Can I make this look like something I know?

Provide for construction play

Along with the many toys geared toward building and construction, try adding unusual collections of open-ended materials to encourage construction. Add a variety of ways to connect things to other things.

Tape. Duct tape, masking tape, electrical tape, cellophane tape, packing tape, colored cloth tape of different widths and colors, sticky dots and squares, file folder labels, stickers of all kinds.

Tools. Hole punch, leather punch, stapler, glue gun, sewing machine, hammer, screwdriver, pliers, wrench.

Connectors. Toothpick, playdough, Styrofoam, straw, yarn, string, clothespin; wire, nail, twist tie, paper clip, thumbtack, rubber band, brad fastener, clip, ring, diaper pin.

Pretend

Role Plays

Diego runs up to the top of the short hill. He drags a long rope behind him. He pretends to have a hard time pulling the rope. "Come on, you big cow!" he says as he grunts and pulls.

Children act out ideas and feelings using props. *They may ask themselves the following questions.*

- What can I make this thing be?
- How can I use this for my role play?
- What can these other things and people become in my play?

Provide for Pretend Role Play

Typical dress-up clothes, pretend housekeeping equipment, and a variety of traditional prop boxes (such as gas station, store, restaurant, hospital, firefighter, and office props) are all important materials for pretend role play. A number of common social and emotional themes also arise during pretend play. Here are some ideas that will enhance these themes.

Birthdays

Children often talk about birthdays, birthday parties, and cakes. These celebrations provide a special ritual and sense of importance and power in childhood. Children use birthday parties as a bargaining chip in negotiating relationships. They will frequently say to one another, "If you let me play, you can be my best friend and come to my birthday."

To build on this popular theme, create a prop box with calendars, growth charts with photos, candles, decorations, cake pans, playdough for the cakes, party favors, hats, boxes, wrapping paper, bows, tape, and materials to make invitations and thank you notes.

As children play, listen to the fascinating ideas and understandings they pursue about friendship, the passage of time, aging, and celebration.

Separation

Separation anxiety is common among young children. Moving away from family into the larger world of preschool and child care is a difficult transition for many children.

Through dramatic play and story time, children can act out their fears and gain understanding and power over separation issues. Make up your own stories using small dramatic play characters and puppets or felt pieces as props. Then leave these out for the children to play with.

Reading books to children and then creating prop boxes or felt pieces related to the stories about separation provide opportunities for children to "play" with these powerful issues. Some good books about separation include *Are You My Mother?* by P. D. Eastman; *The Runaway Bunny* by Margaret Wise Brown; *Mama, Do You Love Me?* by Barbara M. Joosse; and *The Leaving Morning* by Angela Johnson.

Children's Fears

Observe children's activities and interactions for themes related to their fears and insecurities. Some children are afraid of monsters or the dark. For many children, hurricanes, earthquakes, floods, and fires are part of an annual cycle. Others experience violence, murder, and stories of gangs and war. Increasingly, children have a firsthand experience with a death in the family.

Children feel helpless and powerless to take care of themselves in the world. The strong popularity of superheroes in the media reflects children's needs to act out powerful, invincible roles. Rather than forbidding superhero play or avoiding scary issues, respond and create curriculum around them. Here are some examples of teacher efforts.

Floods

Barb's child care program is right next to a river that had its one-hundred-year flood while she and the children watched. For weeks, the children observed helicopters landing with sandbags and volunteers fighting to keep the river back.

The children's play reflected what they were seeing each day. They used books and blocks to build the dike and took turns pretending to be the river that broke through. Barb added helicopters, small people figures, and picture books about rivers and floods. She transferred these props to the water table and added some sand. Floods became the theme of their play for weeks.

Earthquakes

After an earthquake shook her community, Sharon and her children took turns building a town with blocks and props on top of a wobbly table. Each time their town was built, they shook the table and watched as the earthquake toppled the buildings. They built and knocked down their town over and over again. Sharon added props to let the children act out the powerful roles of medics, firefighters, and construction workers.

Power Stories

Watching superhero play all week in his class, Tom approached a small group of children with a pen and a homemade blank book he keeps for these occasions. He sat near the play and asked the children to tell him their power stories.

As the children talked, he wrote what they said. "I'm the strongest one in the world," said Anthony. "I can even pick up houses. Laser beams come out of my eyes and turn people to stone and ice. Then they go to sleep forever." The other children joined in, adding their ideas to the power story.

Soon the aggressive play had changed to an engaged, meaningful discussion. The children cooperatively designed costumes and props to build on their story themes.

Tom read the power stories later during circle time. He noticed that all the children were as engrossed in the stories as those who created them. He sought out his co-workers for more ideas on how to work with the power theme.

Games

Jessica and Ryan balance long blocks vertically in one corner of the block area. From the other side they roll cylinder-shaped blocks toward these long blocks. As blocks are knocked down, they remind each other of the score and whose turn is next.

Children agree on a set of rules to follow for a game. *As they play they ask themselves all sorts of questions.*

- Can I play a game with these?
- What rules are needed for this game?
- How can we make this game more fun?

Provide for Games

In addition to commercial games (evaluate these games to be certain that they are non-biased, inclusive, gender fair and promote cooperation), stock the classroom with a supply of props for child-created games. Watch for opportunities to offer these to children when they seem engaged in a game-play theme.

Game Props

Following are some suggestions:

- ball, cylinder, beanbag, large cardboard
- spinner, dice, coin for taking turns
- watches, clock, and timer for taking turns
- chart paper, clipboard, and paper and pens for making lists and keeping score
- pictures, photographs, blank cards, boxes, and cardboard for game boards that can be created and played over and over.

Meaningful Work Themes

Children love to be involved with real work; they want to help carry, fix, cook, build, wash, plan, and organize things. They develop a strong identity, a sense of both independence and interdependence when they participate in activities that contribute to their family and classroom community. Providing for this kind of involvement is a critical component of a child-centered curriculum.

Clean-Up Kits

Let children do the real cleaning, vacuuming, and washing. Provide readily accessible materials and encouragement for children to participate. They love to help clean up and sweep the floor using child-sized brooms and dustpans, dust busters, and vacuum cleaners.

Provide spray bottles and sponges for cleaning tables; window cleaner, squeegees, and paper towels for washing windows and tubs; and buckets, sponges, soap, and dish towels for washing dishes, tables, furniture, and toys.

Mealtime Preparation and Set Up

Setting the table, serving food, and cleaning up afterward are all valuable tasks. Rather than just an occasional cooking project, plan and provide regular ways for children to help select and prepare food.

Classroom Maintenance, Repair, and Replacements

Have a tool kit so children can help tape ripped books and bindings and fix an appliance or toy. As materials need replacing, have children participate in selecting and ordering things to be purchased. Together read the instructions and make a plan for regular maintenance.

Lesson Planning and Recording

Have children participate in planning, preparing, and documenting your curriculum. Conduct discussions with them about who is learning what. Involve them in collecting samples of their work and dictated words. Collect photo displays of what has been happening in the classroom and display them. Involve the children in selecting things for their individual portfolios.

Helping Your Classmates

As much as possible, refer children to each other for help. They can assist each other in learning how to zip, tie, and use a toy or a tool. They can offer comfort and help to someone in need. Rather than just a jobs chart, a classroom helper's chart could be a skills bank or a resource map for regular referral.

Physical Development Themes

Unlike adults who can pretend that their bodies are inconsequential, children bring their bodies with them wherever they go. Teachers can often be found reminding children to use "inside voices" or "walking feet," and to sit "crisscross applesauce." These teachers tend to treat outdoor play as a time to burn off steam rather than a way to build bodies. Many female teachers, socialized to have their bodies seen and not developed, often neglect children's physical development themes.

Most children are kinesthetic learners and need to move around as a way of paying attention and learning. For these and other children, provide for active bodies in your classroom, don't just tolerate them.

Body Themes

Simple materials and equipment—offered daily both indoors and outdoors—encourage the kind of physical movement so important for children's development. If creeping and crawling is the curriculum theme for the day, then the materials and activities you offer should provide for these skills. For example, you might set up obstacle courses using blankets and tables to make tunnels and large boxes with cutout passageways to explore.

Here are some more ideas for materials and activities to enhance and challenge moving bodies.

Props for Active Bodies

- Pillows and mattresses to build with, hide under, jump on, or rest on.
- Wagons, carts, buckets, boxes, and heavy things to lift and move.
- Balls, beanbags, balloons, and bubbles to chase, reach and jump for, pound, pop, and swing at.
- Steps, ladders, trees, wooden planks, sheets, blankets, and large spools to build ever-changing and challenging places to climb, jump, and hide.
- Mirrors to see yourself and your body moving.
- Shovels, ropes, and pulleys for building and inventing.
- Riding toys, bikes, trikes, roller skates, and push and pull toys for negotiating speed, balance, and terrain and transporting materials and people from place to place.
- Milk cartons, cardboard tubes, and inner tubes, rope, and other loose parts to build and invent with.
- Large mounds or hills of dirt, grass and sand, grassy fields, bushes, trees, water, holes, tunnels, and hiding places to experience the sensory joys and the physical challenges that only nature can provide.

Movements You See	Materials and Activities to Offer
pushing pulling scooting	
running dancing marching chasing	
retrieving carrying loading unloading lifting digging hiding	
pounding knocking down throwing picking up balancing	
bouncing jumping kicking pedaling swinging	

Now it's your turn to practice. Here are more body movements you might see children exploring. Look over the list and in the space provided brainstorm possible materials and activities you could provide.

Creative Expression Themes

Traditional early childhood creative expression curriculum (including art, music, and block building) usually involves a product. Teachers plan projects for children to make, or ask questions about what the children are making rather than what they are doing. Look for the process themes children go through during these creative activities. These themes reveal developmental stages that are usually more important than a final product.

Stages of Creative Expression

Exploring. As in other play arenas, children begin creative expression activities by exploring the property of materials. They examine, manipulate, experiment, and repeatedly try things. This exploration is an important step in learning to use materials for representing ideas and feelings.

Exploring behavior leading to creative expression may look something like the following:

- Block building: Knocking down structures created by others; carrying blocks around and putting them down in specific places; experimenting with connecting and stacking blocks.
- Painting: Smearing paint and tasting it; using hands to paint with; painting one's body; dabbing with a brush; painting lines similar to scribbles; covering whole areas of the paper with paint.

- Using playdough: Tasting and eating dough; pinching, squeezing, and pounding dough or clay; rolling to make coils and balls.

Naming. As children explore and use materials, they begin to notice something they want to name. You've probably seen examples like these:

- Block building: As Tamara continues stacking and connecting, she says, "I made a house."
- Painting: As Jasmine uses big arm movements to smear the green paint back and forth across the paper, she exclaims, "I'm making a tree."
- Using playdough: Making balls, coils, and other forms, Jamal talks of snakes, pancakes, cars, and birthday cakes.

Representing. As children learn to explore and use tools, they intentionally begin to create representations. Their representations include props for pretending and role-playing, along with art and construction creations. Unlike teacher-planned arts and crafts that represent adult views, however, children's creative products represent their own thinking and learning—which are often complex and significant.

Consider the skills and ideas these children express:

- *Block building:* Taiko has a small hamster at home. Today at preschool, she announces her plans to build a house for the hamster in the block area. She finds the block shapes she wants to use and builds an initial structure with long corridors and small cove-like areas. She says, "This is for my hamster to run through. And these places are for food so he can stop to eat whenever he gets hungry." She goes searching for more shapes to add to her already complex piece of architecture.

- *Painting:* Gabrielle spends the whole morning at the art table making pictures of her family. She adds more color and detail to each one, and includes a slightly different emphasis to distinguish them. She says to her friend, "Here we are eating dinner," and, "Here's a picture of me and my mom in our backyard. See, my mom, Jacquie, just cut the grass so it doesn't hide the mosquitoes."
- *Using playdough:* Sam and Jacob are working with the playdough and a set of plastic dishes and pans. They are cooking dinner using the playdough as the food. "Let's have hamburgers for our dinner," says Sam. "Okay," answers Jacob. "I'll make the burgers and you make the buns." They work together and create an elaborate representation with the playdough, including blobs for the ketchup and snake shapes for the French fries.

Provide for Creative Expression

Are you limiting paint to only two or three color choices at the easel? Do you stop the children from mixing the paint and the paint brushes? Do you offer only predesigned art projects for children to copy?

Providing for creative expression to meet the underlying developmental themes that children are exploring means providing for processes, not products. Set up your art and sensory areas to include an array of open-ended materials to combine and transform. Plan for and allow the variety of approaches and uses that each child will bring to the creative process.

Painting Activities

Think about painting as a process for exploration rather than for an end product. Plan and provide ways for children to experiment with painting by offering a variety of paper and other objects to paint on, an array of implements to paint with, and different substances and textures to use as paint. Choose from the following lists of ideas to have available in your art area. Be sure you offer a number of choices, not just one or two.

Paper to use:
- adding machine tape, envelopes
- bags and boxes of all sizes and shapes
- cardboard, butcher paper, computer paper, construction paper
- wrapping paper, wallpaper, greeting cards
- coffee filters, foil, waxed paper, sandpaper, Styrofoam
- folders, index cards, junk mail

Substances to paint with:
- tempera paint, watercolor, fingerpaint, food coloring
- glass wax, liquid starch, condensed milk, salt, flour
- mud, soap flakes, shaving cream
- glue, white and colored
- water
- textures to add to paint: sugar, sand, cornmeal, glitter, extracts

Objects to paint with:
- brushes of all kinds: scrub brush, vegetable brush, bottle brush, toothbrush, hairbrush, paint brush,

> Providing for creative expression to meet the underlying developmental themes that children are exploring means providing for processes not products.

barbecue grill brush, make-up brush, whisk broom, feather duster, nail brush
- kitchen items of all kinds: potato masher, baster, cookie cutter, sponge, scouring pad, chopsticks, berry basket, egg carton, jar lid, fly swatter, straw, rolling pin, cork, candle, toothpick
- items from nature: pinecone, leaf, evergreen bough, flower, corncob, rock, shell, feather, sunflower, twig, branch
- miscellaneous items: sponge brushes and rollers of all sizes, string, yarn, rope, toy car, eyedropper, squeeze bottle, spray bottle, marble, plastic golf ball, spool, carpet piece, cotton, Q-tip cotton swabs, spun wool

Objects to paint on:
- paper, box, linoleum, fabric
- rock, shell
- wood, twig, branch, brick, tile
- glass, mirror, metal, can, bottle
- bag, plate, basket, tray, pan
- body, hand, foot, face

Transformation Activities

Children are spellbound by activities and materials they can manipulate, change, and transform. They are drawn to activities that involve all their senses because using their senses is the way they learn about the world. Through these kinds of activities, children observe, make predictions, and develop problem-solving skills. They learn about the world of science, physics, and mathematics in appropriate, hands-on ways. Stretch your comfort level with messiness and plan for these popular activities with children.

Magical Potions.

Think bigger than the traditional water table and sandbox. Provide children with exciting materials that change and grow as they mix and shake. Add pitchers, containers, and utensils to tubs or the sensory table with the following materials and then sit back and watch children discover the following:

- flour and water get sticky and gooey like glue
- flour dough with yeast rises, grows, and smells terrific
- vinegar and baking soda smoke and fizzle
- warm milk, food coloring, and dish soap magically swirl together
- cornstarch and water become a goopy substance that stays firm when you squeeze it, but drips when you open your hand
- glue, water, and borax mixed together become a blubbery substance that stretches when you hold it and makes bubbles when you blow it
- blocks of ice, laced with food coloring, transform to colorful ice caves when rock salt is poured on top
- plain dirt and water create that ever so delightful substance—mud!

Life Cycle Observations.

The natural change of the seasons and all of the living things of the world are wonderful transformation processes to observe together. Provide these opportunities throughout your curriculum. Go hunting for them in your yard or neighborhood.

- hatching baby chicks from eggs
- composting food to use as fertilizer for a garden
- growing a garden together, watching things go from seed to flower to fruit and back to the compost
- observing and documenting someone's pregnancy
- documenting the children's own life cycle using photos from home, from infancy to the present; design charts for measuring children's growth in height and weight
- watching caterpillars spin their cocoons and hatch into butterflies; creating a special ritual to set them free (caterpillars can be mail-ordered)
- observing and documenting the changing seasons: keeping track of the light and dark together; measuring the temperature changes and the differences in your clothing and daily lives together; collecting items from nature that reflect the changes

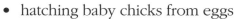

Learning Skills

As children become interested in representing their ideas and experiences, they need more skills to accomplish their plans. They may seek help in using tools to make what they have in mind.

Many teachers are uncertain of their role in teaching skills to young children. Some try to do so before children show interest or have a meaningful context for learning the skill. This usually causes frustration and feelings of failure. Other teachers avoid teaching skills, thinking a child-centered approach means no direct instruction. If children have no skills to carry out their ideas, this, too, can result in frustration and failure.

When children are ready to learn, they need to serve as an apprentice with a mentor or coach. Helpful instructions, demonstrations, and breaking down tasks for skill building are appropriate teacher interventions.

- Robert has used playdough to make all of the parts of a dog: a body, four legs, and a head. He is having trouble firmly connecting the parts so the dog will stand up. He asks Miss Williams, "Will you fix my dog for me?"
- Rebecca tells the teacher, "I want to paint a picture of a butterfly. Will you help me?"
- Masayo is making a tall tower with the blocks. She has been working to connect two towers with a bridge. Each time she tries, the towers fall over.

A Closer Look

One of the golden rules of early childhood education is to encourage children to do things for themselves. The underlying goal of this rule is to help children feel capable and proud of what they can do on their own. As adults, we have been warned to avoid models for children to copy so that they will not compare their lesser efforts to ours. However, in the above scenarios, a teacher following these rules would miss the developmental nature of these children's requests.

Robert needs help to accomplish his goal of putting the dog together. He's thought through his ideas and come up with a representation himself. Rather than leaving him to figure it out for himself, the teacher can offer support by asking questions, making suggestions, and a giving a helping hand if needed. For example, the teacher might demonstrate how she would attach one of the body parts and let him finish the rest.

Read through the following scenarios and think about how you might respond to these children.

Rebecca may know what butterflies look like and even have an idea about one she would like to paint. The teacher assesses her needs and helps Rebecca explore her ideas with probing questions and suggestions. Rebecca might also benefit from looking through picture books and magazines with photographs of butterflies and butterfly paintings to help her formulate her representation. The teacher might offer a demonstration of how to use paint so Rebecca can get the results she is after.

Masayo also would fare better with some questions and suggestions for analyzing what is happening as she builds so that she might try other approaches.

In each case, the teacher needs to carefully observe and analyze what the child is trying to achieve and serve as a scaffold to overcome the challenges by coaching, modeling, and teaching skills.

Practice Responding
to Children's Themes

Samantha's project

Samantha is working in the carpentry area. She uses the vise to measure and saw pieces of wood about six inches long. Then she uses that piece to measure and cut another piece the same size. Removing the wood from the vise, she places the two cut pieces on top of each other and, with two hands, begins hammering a nail through the top piece. She hits the nail head every third or fourth try and periodically stops to reposition the wood, which slides around the table. When she

To practice applying the ideas and skills in this chapter, read each of the following projects and decide which responses involve a child-centered approach.

realizes the nail isn't attaching the two pieces together, she leaves the area. The next time you notice her, she's back in the carpentry area with a bottle of glue. Having attached the two pieces of wood together, she is now gluing some Styrofoam circles on the side.

1. What developmental themes are apparent in Samantha's play? From your observation, describe her approach to learning, the ideas she is exploring, and the skills she is using and practicing.

2. What role is the teacher playing in making one of the following responses? How might Samantha feel or interpret this response? Does this response help the teacher learn more about Samantha? Consider these questions as you evaluate the following five possible teacher responses:

a. The teacher says, "Oh, what a nice car you are making."
b. The teacher says, "I noticed how you used the vise to hold the wood while you measured and sawed."
c. The teacher says, "There's some paint in the art area. Would you like to paint your car?"
d. The teacher asks, "How many wheels does a car need?"
e. The teacher stands back and watches to see what Samantha is going to do next.

3. What response would you like to see happen?

Did you notice that the teacher response with descriptive language (b) is the most pertinent to the child's interest? The other statements and questions (responses a, c, and d) almost seem trivial and simplistic. When is it appropriate for a teacher to watch

A Closer Look

and say nothing as reflected in the last description? If a teacher observes with a purpose, she or he gathers more information for curriculum planning and appropriate interventions in the future.

Mario's Project

Mario seems to be enjoying himself in the sand area. He started filling a baby bottle first using his hand as a scoop and then using a cup as a scoop. He then turned the baby bottle over and used it as a scoop. Now he is using a funnel as a scoop and noticing that the sand can run out both ends of the funnel into the bottle.

1. What developmental themes are apparent in Mario's play? From your observation, describe his approach to learning, the ideas he is exploring, and the skills he is using and practicing.

2. What role is the teacher playing in making one of the following responses? How might Mario feel or interpret this response? Does this response help the teacher learn more about Mario? Consider these questions as you evaluate the following five possible teacher responses:

> a. The teacher picks up a bigger funnel and asks, "Which of these funnels is bigger, yours or mine?"
> b. The teacher picks up a funnel and tries using it just like Mario and thinks to herself, "Maybe if I get a container and funnel and use them the same way he does, Mario will talk to me about his play."
> c. The teacher says to Mario, "You figured out how to get sand into that bottle two different ways!"
> d. The teacher says, "Mario, are you making a birthday cake?"

e. The teacher says, "Mario, why don't you pour your sand over this truck and bury it?"

3. What response would you like to see happen?

Responses b and c take into consideration Mario's interests at the sand table. Often a teacher's ideas and interest have no meaning to the child (for example, responses a, d, and e). Following the child's lead starts to impact the way one responds.

A Closer Look

LaToya's Project

LaToya seems to be hanging around the edges of the dress-up corner beauty parlor play as if she would like to join in. She is holding a purse and some rollers and is watching the "beauty parlor lady" and the girl in the chair getting her hair done.

1. What developmental themes are apparent in LaToya's play? From your observation, describe her approach to learning, the ideas she is exploring, and the skills she is using and practicing.

2. What role is the teacher playing in making one of the following responses? How might LaToya feel or interpret this response? Does this response help the teacher learn more about LaToya? Consider these questions as you evaluate the following five possible teacher responses:

a. The teacher says to the other children, "LaToya wants to play. Why don't you be nice and invite her to play with you?"

b. The teacher thinks to herself, "Maybe if I get a purse and some rollers I could say, 'Hi, I'd sure like to get my hair fixed too.' I'll wait to see if LaToya wants to keep watching or if she wants to join in the play."

A Closer Look

c. The teacher says, "I see you have a purse and some rollers with you. Are you going to fix the doll's hair?"

d. The teacher says, "Only four people are allowed in the dress-up area, LaToya. You'll have to find somewhere else to play until someone leaves this area."

e. The teacher says, "Hey, beauty parlor lady, you have another customer waiting for her appointment."

3. What response would you like to see happen?

Responses b, c, and e coach while still allowing LaToya to take the necessary steps to join the play. Coaching gives the teacher an opportunity to observe and encourage involvement but still respect the child's preferences and intentions.

About Your

Theme Planning

Use this page to reflect on your use of themes in your curriculum planning. These questions will get you started.

Does your current planning provide for the children's developmental themes or only topical themes?

What changes would you like to make?

Our School's Not Fair:
A Story About

Emergent Curriculum

Ann Pelo,
Preschool Teacher

Early one fall, after several days of fierce debate about the differences between steam shovels and excavators, my class of nine four year olds visited the library, hoping to find answers to our questions. On our way back to our child care center, arms full of books about construction, we passed a church with a wheelchair accessible parking sign at the curb. One of the children asked why the sign was there and what it meant. To answer her questions, we examined the church, found a matching sign on the only door without stairs, and concluded that the door with the wheelchair sign was especially for people with wheelchairs who are not able to use stairs. The parking sign, the children figured out, saved a parking place for people who need to use the door without stairs.

In our discussion about the church and its signs, a child commented that our school (which is housed upstairs in another church building) was unfair because "We have too many stairs." Another child, Sophie, told us about her stepfather who uses a wheelchair and who is unable to come into our school to pick her up or visit her. She told us that they have a ramp at their house for him to use. Several children exclaimed, "We need to build a ramp at our school!"

There on the sidewalk, late for lunch, arms heavy with books, faces sure and excited, the children challenged me to listen attentively and throw in my hat with them. "This is for serious," one of the children stated, and I was with them: We would try to build a ramp at our school.

Here's a story that infuses anti-bias principles into an emergent curriculum. It is a sustained project built on the topical themes of ramps and wheelchairs and the developmental themes of construction and fairness.

During the walk back to school and through lunch, we created a list of what we might need to build a ramp; I encouraged the children to think of steps we would need to take before we could plunge into the actual building. And then it was naptime. I caught my breath and reviewed what had happened. I was embarking on a journey with the children. My responsibilities during this journey involved careful balancing of two seemingly contrary tasks: (1) attentive listening to the children; watching them for cues about their interests, skills, questions, and knowledge; and responding to what I heard and saw; and (2) introducing ideas, initiating exploration, and leading the children into new territory. These are the challenges of emergent curriculum for me: responding and anticipating, following and initiating.

During naptime on that first day, I wrote a note to the parents in my class, explaining what we'd embarked on. I began talking with my co-workers, my director, and our center's trainer, alerting people to this emerging curriculum focus on accessibility. I asked for resources, thoughts, and support.

I also sketched a curriculum web with "wheelchair accessibility/ramp building" in the center. This made tangible the challenge of following while leading. This initial web, I knew, must not become "the curriculum plan for the month" if our accessibility project was to remain responsive to the children's discoveries, questions, and passions. Instead, this web would serve as a way to focus my thinking, to generate ideas for stocking the classroom environment with props, and to prepare for the surprises that would come from the children and their families as we pursued this project. In my thinking about emergent curriculum, I see this initial web more as a guidebook for traveling, with reminders to "Be ready for...," "Be sure to spend some time at...," and "Bring along...." This web would not be a map marked in red to be followed unwaveringly.

And so I stocked the environment with building materials, seriation and classification games using nuts and bolts, ramp-shaped blocks, and books about construction and people using wheelchairs. I borrowed a wheelchair and brought in a persona doll in a wheelchair. These wheelchairs led us to accessibility issues about our classroom: Children used the chair during our daily meetings, and noticed how different our meeting circle looked; they used the wheelchair during work time and found that they couldn't reach the lowest shelves in our room; they tried to use the wheelchair to go to the bathroom, and discovered that they couldn't get through the door. We rearranged the room and added the bathroom doors to our building plans. Children wanted Carmella, the persona doll, to come to lunch with us, but our lunchroom is downstairs and so she remained upstairs in our classroom alone each day—and the children's passion for our project was strengthened.

As we began this accessibility project, I invited parents to join us, contributing resources, time, and interest. Several parents who are architects brought in architectural drawings, which were soon scattered around the room as children pored over them and began integrating them into their drawings. A family in our class who had recently remodeled their home brought in a mound of photos tracing their project step-by-step, and another family invited us to visit their torn-up attic as they began a rewiring project.

This effort toward parental involvement was difficult, highlighting some of the differences between the culture of Reggio Emilia and the affluent, professional, European-American culture in which my child care center is situated. It was an effort to get parents to read notes, listen to stories, bring in resources, leave work to come on a trip with us, invite us to their homes, and transform their contact with school from drop off/pick up to one of community involvement. It was an effort for me to let go of my position as the only adult in the classroom and be ready to add to or change my ideas, to truly welcome parents' involvement.

Early in our accessibility project, the children and I began a dialogue with members of the church with whom we share space. The children dictated a letter to the building committee, explaining that "our school is not fair" and that we hoped to build a ramp to make it more fair. The committee chairperson contacted me to say that the church had explored the possibility of building a ramp and a wheelchair lift several years earlier and had found the cost and remodeling effort involved to be more than they could undertake. I asked for support from the church for my class' project, despite their prior decision not to go ahead with a ramp, advocating for the children's learning and experience with activism. I felt both sheepish, in the face of their carefully researched decision, and fiercely determined to move ahead with this project, championing the children's right to try. The church committee agreed to send a person to meet with our class and gave us the thumbs up on our project.

Through all this, the children practiced using building tools, working long and hard at the workbench and mastering the use of hammers, saws, and drills. Children began using models and drawings to guide and represent their block building, extending their work with the architectural drawings. I invited an architect to visit and tour our school with us; she drew our attention to the concepts of slope and ramp length.

During these weeks, we took the wheelchair on trips through the neighborhood and, often, to Sophie's house, where her dad gave children rides on his wheelchair, up and down the ramp at his house. We sketched his ramp and crafted models of it to use back at school in our project. On these trips through the neighborhood, children became increasingly frustrated as they encountered sidewalks without ramps and suggested, in their passion about unfairness, that we tell the people who make sidewalks that they must build ramps—and we did. The children dictated a letter that we sent to the city engineering department, and so we began a dialogue with one of the pedestrian safety engineers. This course of activism was not in my initial web; it was one of the surprises the children offered me during this project. Our correspondence led to several visits by the safety engineer, culminating many months later in a trip she organized for us to a neighborhood site where a sidewalk ramp was being poured; the children helped arrange the frames and smooth the wet cement. They called this ramp "their ramp" for the rest of the year.

Through all of this, I took many photos; made and kept copies of the children's letters to the church, city, and their parents; and tape recorded conversations among the children and transcribed them. I wanted to create a record of our project, our classroom history, as it developed. I used the photos, letters, and tape recordings to look and listen closely to the children and plan from their concerns, passions, and understandings. The children used the documentation as a common frame of reference, and would often take out the "Ramp Book" (a photo album) and tell each other the stories of the photos and letters in it.

We did not build a ramp at our school. The church committee's early advice proved true: The cost and amount of remodeling required were more than we could manage. I still, in some ways, feel this as a failure. "A Reggio school would have built the ramp," I say to myself, though I understand the many differences between my school and the Reggio schools.

The successes of this project, though, are manifold. I learned much about the challenges and value of making space and time for learning to unfold, and began my work toward genuinely inviting parents into the life of the classroom. This four-month project assured me that listening to the children is my best guide for curriculum planning. This project began as a debate about construction machinery and became a passionate effort to remedy unfairness; it was sustained by the children's passion and excitement and investment in making our school fair, and by careful listening and planning that honored their passion and interests.

The children reminded me through the year of the power this project had in their lives. Through the rest of the year, each building they made with blocks, each house they drew, had a ramp, carefully designed for accessibility. On each field trip we took the children noted the wheelchair accessible parking places, becoming indignant and angry when someone parked inappropriately. And I continue to hear from their kindergarten teachers and their families about these children's awareness of fairness issues, particularly accessibility issues, and about their surety that they ought to act for fairness.

Caring for
Infants and Toddlers

Infant and toddler

caregivers are involved

with one of the most

amazing and rapidly

developing times of

the human experience.

5

Today, infant caregivers Helen and Sherrial find a rare minute to sit and talk. Baby Ruby sucks on a toy, watching Sherrial fold diapers on the floor beside her. In the rocking chair, Helen gives Louis his bottle. The other babies are all asleep. **"Our curriculum plans** are due again tomorrow, aren't they?" sighs Helen. "What shall we do? It's April. Maybe we should cut out umbrellas and raindrops to put on the wall." "Whatever," responds Sherrial. "I always feel stupid trying to make up curriculum plans for babies." **Seeing** Sherrial's disgruntled face, Ruby begins kicking her feet, frowning, and making sounds. **"Look at you,** Ruby, you've got something to say about this too. Here, come sit with Miss Sherrial and tell us what your curriculum should be."

What's the Curriculum?

Caregivers who have school on their mind may find that thinking about curriculum for infants and toddlers is a challenge. They think, what do Valentines or shamrocks mean to a toddler or April umbrellas to an infant? And these caregivers are right—these are school themes. Yet these themes are often the only framework caregivers have for dutifully trying to meet requirements for curriculum plans. Although she might not realize it, Miss Sherrial has the right idea. Interactive responses to cues is what curriculum for toddlers and infants is all about.

Read the scenario again. Notice how Baby Ruby follows what her caregiver is doing. When she sees Miss Sherrial's face and hears the new tone in her voice, Ruby becomes worried. She communicates this with the language of her body and voice. Miss Sherrial lets Ruby know her message was received and responds with a comforting lap.

Infant and toddler caregivers are involved with one of the most amazing and rapidly developing times of the human experience. It is a time when children are most acutely learning who they are, from adults and from their interactions and responses to them. Infant and toddler caregivers have a remarkable impact on this process.

As Ron Lally, director of the Infant and Toddler Training Program of the Far West Laboratory in California, describes it:

"In infant and toddler caregiving, more is happening than tender loving care and learning games—values and beliefs are being witnessed and incorporated. The way you act is perceived, interpreted, and incorporated into the actual definition of the self the child is forming."

Relationships

Are the Curriculum

For infants and toddlers, responsive interactions are what curriculum is about. Usually we don't think about responding to babies as a plan, but rather do it at a subconscious level. We act and react—to a child's body movement, facial expression, and a certain cry or giggle. We change a wet diaper and feed a hungry belly. Often we do all of this without a second thought, without noticing the complexity of what is involved in these brief, ordinary exchanges. But when we look closely at what is happening and its significance, the ordinary becomes extraordinary.

In the caregiving relationship, infants and toddlers are learning who they are and what they are capable of in each of these small moments with adults. The children are subconsciously searching for answers to questions such as:

- Is the world a safe place?
- Will my needs be met?
- Am I a successful communicator?
- Can I get my message across?
- Will you accept my raw, uncensored emotions?

These are critical issues of trust, which is a primary theme for this stage of development. Other big themes for this time of life include autonomy, separation and control:

- Can I meet my own needs?
- Do I have any power?
- If we part, will you still be there?

As a caregiver, your job is to learn about the developmental needs and tasks of this age group while you come to know each child's individual way of being and expressing herself or himself. Equally important, you must learn to know yourself so you are conscious of your reactions and can intentionally respond to enhance the well-being and self-concept of each child who depends on you.

The following sections include exercises to help build your awareness and skills for a truly child-centered infant and toddler curriculum.

Use Children's Books

Looking through picture books about infants can remind toddler and infant caregivers of how to think about curriculum for this age group—and how to interact with this age group in culturally sensitive ways.

For example, *On the Day I Was Born* by Deborah Chocolate (Scholastic, 1995) has illustrations and language that immediately remind the reader of the themes of softness, a sense of belonging, and being the center of attention and delight of everyone's eye. How can you plan for these themes in your child care program?

Another good example is *Welcoming Babies* by Margy Burns Knight (Tilbury House, 1994). This book shows the different ways cultural traditions convey a sense of identity and affinity to young children.

Examine the elements in this book to enlighten your caregiving practices.

Analyzing books written for toddlers can give you insight into the developmental themes and tasks these children are exploring. Two examples are by Margaret Wise Brown—both of which hold toddlers spellbound.

Goodnight Moon (Harper, 1947) has simple, clear pictures and text, naming familiar objects over and over again. Children are drawn to the familiarity of the objects and the predictability of the text. This fascination is consistent with their need for safety and trust in their environment and daily routines.

The Runaway Bunny (Harper, 1942) portrays the intense themes of trust and autonomy as the little bunny asserts her will and independence by climbing mountains and sailing away, only to have her mother assure her that she will always come after her.

Another recommended book is *Mama, Do You Love Me?* by Barbara Joosse (Chronicle Books, 1991). This book is a version of the runaway bunny story told within a particular cultural framework. As with Margaret Wise Brown's book, it is also alive with the intense emotions young ones are experiencing: If I have a big tantrum, even if I'm naughty, will you still love me?

Be on the lookout for other books that hold children's attention time and time again. As you read through them, ask yourself these questions:

- What do the pictures and colors depict?
- How would I describe the language and rhythm of the text?
- What are the underlying themes of the story?
- How does this book relate to a developmental issue or task in children?
- How can I include these elements in my caregiving environment and routines?

Make Friends with a Baby

Your intuition often provides a wealth of understanding about child-centered curriculum for infants and toddlers. Try the following activity with a partner or group of co-workers to help you recognize and name your current knowledge and skills.

On a sheet of paper, create three columns with the following headings: How do you make friends with a baby?; Why does this work?; and What does the baby offer in return?

With your group, brainstorm a list of answers for each heading. Be specific. Push yourself to describe more details.

Draw a line under your last entry in each column. Now think about how you can make friends with a toddler, why this works, and what is offered by them.

Look over the lists you made to find answers to these questions:

- What are the characteristics and needs of children of this age?
- What are responsive caregiving roles and interactions for these needs?
- What skills and know-how do infants and toddlers already have?
- How can I use this information to think about curriculum for infants and toddlers?
- What are the sources of interest and reward I find in working with infants and toddlers?
- Can I develop any affirmations from this list to sustain me in my work?

Reading and Responding to Cues

With infants and toddlers, interactions in the caregiving process are primarily based on nonverbal cues. Adults send and receive hundreds of messages in our daily interactions through facial expressions and our tone of voice. This form of communication, although subtle and at a subconscious level, is extremely powerful. The way we move our bodies, tilt our heads, and touch and hold a child tells her or him about themselves and the world around them.

Try the following activities to enhance your awareness of the cues you read and send in working with infants and toddlers.

Analyze Pictures

Gather a collection of photographs of infants and toddlers in various activities from magazines, newspapers, and books. Practice reading cues and analyzing responses by looking at each photo and asking yourself the following questions.

- How does this picture make me feel?
- What do I think this child needs?
- How do I know this?
- What would my response and specific behavior be with this child?

How do you think the child in the photograph would perceive your responses? Consider these questions from the child's perspective:

- How successful are my messages to this person?

- How interesting am I?
- Are my feelings understood and acceptable?
- Is it safe to be myself?
- What should I fear?

Observe Interactions Between Adults and Children

In a store, restaurant, or shopping mall, use the questions above to analyze a five-minute observation between a baby or toddler and an adult.

After practicing with photos and other children and adults, use the above questions to analyze an interaction of your own with a child in your care.

Principles for Reading and Responding to Children's Cues

As you continue to develop your ability to read and respond to infant and toddler cues, keep the following points in mind.

Observe. What nonverbal message is the child sending? From the child's point of view, what is she or he trying to communicate? Consider body language and tone of voice.

Assess. Wait before you respond. Try to determine what is influencing your feelings about what the child is doing. Look at your own body language to assess what it is communicating. Is your message a useful one for the child?

Accept. Whether or not you agree with or like what the child is communicating, use body language to acknowledge you understand what she or he is trying to tell you.

Support. Help the child meet her or his needs or accomplish what she is trying in a safe, acceptable manner.

Everyday Routines

Are the Curriculum

The caregiving process is central to infant and toddler curriculum because it fosters a child's development and positive identity. The more you increase your awareness that everyday materials, activities, and routines constitute a curriculum, the more you will value this idea and help others to see it.

Use the following activity to practice recognizing and describing that everyday actions are important.

Analyze Catalog Materials

Gather several early childhood catalogs and look through the sections related to infants and toddlers. Cut out pictures of materials and routines that are a part of your daily work.

On a sheet of paper, make four columns with the following headings: Material or Activity; What Happens Here?; Social/Emotional Learning; and Sensory/Motor Learning.

Paste the picture or write the name of the object or equipment under the "Material or Activity" column. Then fill in answers under each of the remaining columns. As an example, look through the following chart and practice by filling in the missing blanks.

Material or Activity	What Happens Here?	Social/ Emotional Learning	Sensory/ Motor Learning
Toddler diaper changing station with steps	Caregiver responds to child's need for diaper change.	Trust is reinforced because adult helps meet child's need.	Help noticing the difference between wet and dry.
	Talks about wet diaper.	Sense of self-worth in getting attention and warm response.	Uses arms and hands to pull up pants.
	Uses warm voice, smile, gentle touch.	Conversation and relationship grows.	Learning to climb stairs.
	Describes what she is doing as she changes diaper.	Autonomy grows with involvement in process.	
	Responds to child's interest.	Child feeling valued and capable.	
	Helps child feel dry diaper.		
	Offers child role in pulling up pants.		
	Helps child walk up & down stairs to diaper station.		

Theme Forms

As you become more aware of the curriculum of everyday caregiving, give it the recognition it deserves.

Toddler Self-Help Curriculum

Things in environment to promote self-help	Routines and Interactions	Observations of efforts children make

Growing Language Curriculum

Things in environment to promote language	Routines and Interactions	Observations of efforts children make

Identity and Self-Esteem Curriculum

Things in environment to promote self-help	Routines and Interactions	Observations of efforts children make

Create curriculum formats with headings like the following and document your observations under the heading in each column.

About Your Current

Approach to Caring

for Infants and

Toddlers

*Use this space
to reflect
on your approach
to caring for infants
and toddlers.
The following
questions will
get you started.*

How can you become more aware of your non-verbal cues to children?

What everyday routines could you turn into a curriculum chart for recording your observations?

What changes would you like to make?

Riding the Waves Again:

A Journal Entry

**About Returning to
Work with Toddlers**

Deb Curtis,
Interim Toddler Teacher

I am working with two year olds again. I haven't had this kind of daily responsibility or relationships with a group of children for about fifteen years. I have a lot of knowledge and understanding of their development and also lots of strategies for working with a group of children, all of which I have deeply constructed through my years of teacher training. It's wonderful to be able to stop and think about what's going on, and wait a while to see what happens. As the weeks go by, my relationships with individual children are forming as I begin to know each of them for who they are. They seem to like me, too! And I think I'm getting quite good again at being with them.

I'm also a bit cautious and clumsy at times. What I am still in the process of relearning is the intuitive nature of the work. There is a physical and emotional rhythm that the group seems to have—at times the children are so engaged and cohesive that the room almost hums with a steady, melodic beat. Then there are moments when it changes to a cacophony of sounds and bodies, all colliding as they move in their individual rhythms. There's not really a way to control it; you can only watch closely and respond accordingly. You have to anticipate what might happen, try to stay one step ahead of them, and follow their lead as events unfold. And you have to do this while staying focused with them in the moment.

This journal conveys an understanding of the caregiver as an improvisational artist.

It reminds me of learning to swim in the ocean. You only master an understanding of the nature of waves by spending quite a bit of time with your body immersed in the experience. You have to be able to anticipate what's going to happen and follow the lead of the waves, but at the same time be totally observant and aware of what's happening with all the elements at each moment. You can never really be in control or change the waves. You just learn to understand how to respond to them. You know when to go over the top because you've missed your opportunity to catch the wave. You learn when to dive under because if you don't the wave will crash on you and send you whirling and twirling with it to the shore. When this happens, you quickly realize that you should just relax and go with it. You also know when you've caught the wave just at the optimum moment to ride smoothly on the crest and land gently in a pool at the bottom. If you try to fight against the waves, rather than learn to respond in these ways, your experience of the ocean is scary and exhausting.

This really does describe the way I've been experiencing relearning to work with a group of two year olds. It's not that I don't take charge when I need to. I was worried that I wouldn't know how to do that again. I quickly remembered how as I was immediately involved in situations where I had to. I guess this thing I'm trying to describe is the part of teaching that isn't about planning or leading, but about learning to stay with the process.

Organizing and Communicating

Your Approach to Curriculum Planning

A child-centered, culturally relevant curriculum approach is grounded in solid theory and research, and it addresses the real basics children need to thrive and succeed.

6

Your director requires you to turn in your curriculum plans for each of the coming months. However, you want to use an emergent child-centered approach, basing your plans on observations of themes in the children's lives and their play. The director reminds you that NAEYC accreditation guidelines call for a year-long plan for your curriculum. How can you meet these requirements with a child-centered, emergent approach? **Wanting to build** your curriculum around the children's themes, you have been carefully observing and listening. So far, no obvious theme to build on has emerged. The children are primarily talking about Power Rangers and you want to discourage, not emphasize, that interest. What should you do? **A parent** comes to you with a newspaper article on a school task force report that says open-ended education is a failure and teachers must get back to the basics. How can you convince her of your approach?

How would you handle the above situations? You know that a child-centered curriculum can work, but everything—and everyone—seems to be working against you.

The approach to child-centered curriculum advocated in this handbook often seems hampered by the framework and expectations of supervisors and parents. There is a great deal of misinformation and blaming about the roots of school failure.

But one fact remains clear: A child-centered, culturally relevant curriculum approach is grounded in solid theory and research, and it addresses the real basics children need to thrive and succeed. The challenge for a child-centered teacher is to get yourself well-organized, and then become articulate with parents and others about what you are doing and why.

Where do you Begin?

When learning to use a child-centered curriculum approach, many teachers have trouble figuring out how and where to start. At first, a child-centered approach sounds like it has no goals or objectives. The idea of following the children's lead creates visions of chaos and confusion. Teachers respond with comments like: "How can I just let the children do what they want?" "What will the parents say?" "The children won't learn anything!"

What you—and other teachers—come to understand is that a child-centered curriculum requires a much more complex view of teaching and learning than a traditional one. An emergent curriculum has as much structure as a teacher-directed approach. The difference is that the source of the structure is the teacher's understanding and responsiveness to the children, rather than a curriculum recipe or set plan. The teacher and the children create the structure and curriculum together.

Co-Creating the Curriculum

We have discovered that, for most teachers, learning to use an emergent curriculum approach is a developmental process. It takes time to:

- **Shift** our view of what curriculum really is;
- **Develop** advanced skills in observing children;
- **Learn** to analyze children's thinking and development to see new levels of complexity;
- **Practice** new skills and try out ideas; and
- **Experience** success that leads to trusting the children and oneself—and the curriculum that is being co-created.

The following descriptions of thematic approaches to emergent curriculum, as well as the stories at the end of each chapter in this handbook, reflect various approaches to child-centered curriculum that providers and teachers have adopted. Some of these professionals have made small, but significant changes in the face of pressures for teacher-directed, academic lessons. Others have moved to complex levels of understanding and sophistication in their planning, assessing, and responding to children's interests and needs.

We encourage you to start where you are comfortable. Maybe you will set aside a specific time of day to focus on the children's interests. While introducing a traditional curriculum theme, you may recognize children are pursuing their own questions, and you may decide to abandon yours in favor of theirs. Perhaps you'll come to integrate an emergent approach throughout your daily routine. Once you begin to work with the children to develop curriculum in this way, your time together will flourish. You'll find a new meaning to the idea of curriculum themes and projects.

Thematic Approaches to Child-Centered Curriculum

As you get ready to read what follows, look back at your self-reflections and assessments in the first five chapters of this handbook. Then consider which of the following approaches to child-centered curriculum represents your current efforts to be a guardian of childhood. Are you satisfied with this approach, or would you like to develop one of the other approaches described?

You might also want to return to these descriptions after you have read all of the teacher stories at the end of each chapter. Continually assess where you are and cultivate a vision of where you would like to be in your approach to curriculum planning. From time to time ask yourself:

- Are there understandings that are still not clear to me?
- Would some additional skills be helpful?
- Who could I use as a role model and mentor?
- Who might I be a mentor and role model for?

Topical Themes

A teacher or provider using the topical themes approach has made a small but significant change in how she or he views curriculum planning. While he may still use a traditional theme-based approach, the themes he plans come from the emerging interests and events in the children's lives throughout the year, rather than from a pre-planned schedule for the year.

For example, the local baseball team might be in the World Series and all of the children and their families are wrapped up in the excitement. The teacher uses a baseball theme to plan activities, projects, and field trips.

Environmental Themes

Observing how the children are using materials in various areas of the room, a provider or teacher using environmental themes regularly adds more materials and activities to enhance their involvement and provide for further exploration.

For example, the teacher notices that the block area is overflowing with children building creations. She adds a variety of different kinds of blocks, building materials, pictures of construction sites, and related props in other parts of the room, such as the art and dress-up areas.

Developmental Themes

Learning more about such things as sensory motor development and the stages of play, the teacher observes the developmental tasks that children are practicing. He then provides more interactions, activities, and materials to scaffold the learning process.

127

For example, the caregiver notices that many of the older babies in his group are pulling themselves up and finding support for learning to walk. He provides structures (i.e., furniture and cushions) for the babies to pull themselves up and hold on to while standing. He also adds sturdy wheeled toys to push and practice walking.

Shifting Themes

The teacher who uses shifting themes follows the children's ideas and interests as they play, providing materials and activities that pick up on and extend the various themes they are pursuing.

For example, when doll play in the house corner begins to include taking care of a sick baby, the teacher adds props for doctor and medical play that sustains this play. Later, to extend this theme, she provide boxes, wheels, and paint in the art area for them to create ambulances and aid cars.

Sustaining Themes

This approach involves a complex form of curriculum where teachers closely observe and analyze children's thinking and actions around a topic of interest and provide a multitude of avenues for the children to explore and construct their understandings around this theme. Teachers in the school of Reggio Emilia refer to this as providing for "the hundred languages of children." Lillian Katz and Sylvia Chard refer to it as the project approach. Teachers facilitate children's long-term involvement in the exploration process and development of thought. The project becomes an arena for many developmental themes and tasks as teachers hypothesize about the significance of what children are pursuing and provide further opportunities for that. Teachers and children are co-creators of the curriculum and projects often last for months. The teacher stories at the end of chapters 4 and 7 describe the complexity involved in this approach to sustaining a curriculum project.

As you develop your approach to child-centered, emergent curriculum, find a planning process that works for you. This involves some way to focus your thinking and generate ideas about possible directions for the curriculum. Then create a method for documenting what actually happens, where the children take the curriculum, how hypotheses get tested, and when ideas begin to take hold.

The next sections offer examples of how to get organized with planning ideas and ways teachers have documented emergent curriculum.

Getting Organized

As you build your curriculum on children's interests and developmental themes, you'll need the following as a foundation for this work:

- A thoughtfully organized, visually pleasing, and inviting learning environment for our classroom.
- A basic schedule and set of routines that provide security and flexibility for children.
- A guiding framework for decision-making about themes to pursue.
- An understanding of new roles, dispositions, and skills for interactions and interventions with children.

The Learning Environment and Routines

- Create a space that supports projects.
- Provide aesthetic materials that evoke the senses, curiosity, and inquiry.
- Structure large blocks of time for investigation and play.
- Surround the children with representations of their lives, home, and classroom community.

A Framework for Deciding on Projects to Pursue

- Identify underlying themes that could evolve into a project.
- Pursue projects that are readily observable to children.
- Develop projects that you can connect from one day to the next.
- Offer many possible ways to pursue this theme or project.

Teacher Roles and Skills to Acquire

- Set the stage.
- Listen and observe.
- Collaborate with colleagues.
- Initiate projects with a "provocation" to capture the children's attention.
- Build on emerging interests and questions.
- Document the learning process inside the project.

A Planning Process

Curriculum comes from many places: observations of children's interests, their families, experiences, and community and seasonal events. It can come from your life as a teacher as well: a passion, hobby, or particular event that has influenced you.

Curriculum may get introduced by something that unfolds in the life of your classroom community or by a provocation you as the teacher offer—something for the children to discover, uncover, investigate, or experiment with. Once the process happens, your primary job is to observe. Asking questions to yourself, rather than to children, will help you follow their lead and offer the resources and support they need.

Here are some **questions** to guide your observations as curriculum is emerging:

- **What** do the children find interesting about this?
- What do they already seem to **know**, accurately or with misconceptions?
- What are their **questions**?
- How could they represent their **understandings**?

A Four-Step Planning Process

The following four steps can serve as a framework for planning a child-centered curriculum.

Step 1: Provision the environment
Provide enough materials and space for children to explore. What props would help children explore a given theme? Consider props for the dress-up, block, art, and table areas. For example, if the theme seems

to be "Caring for Babies," you might provision with baby dolls, blankets, and beds. Creating a provocation or sparking an interest might mean a visit from a newborn baby, a pregnant mother, or a tape of a crying baby placed in the home center.

As the children become involved with the initial materials, careful observation will assist you in planning your next steps. Use the following questions to gain more information:

- What do the children do with what is provided?
- What about the materials seems fun and pleasurable to the children?
- What themes do they talk about and represent?
- What experiences, people, and objects are in their play?
- What are the children inventing, questioning, or understanding?

Step 2: Sustain the play

Once children are absorbed in a play theme, you can do several things to sustain the activity. For example, with the "Caring for Babies" theme, you can provide more props—a bottle, highchair, car seat, bathing tub, stroller, sling, snugglie, Gerry carrier, and an array of photographs. Try limiting your further participation to asking open-ended questions, making leading statements, and helping them to negotiate problem-solving and conflict resolution to keep the play going.

Observe again while asking yourself the following questions for cues to enrich the play theme and the children's learning:

- What other materials might the children use to extend their experience or represent their ideas and feelings?
- What additional project activities could be

provided to extend or branch out from the children's ideas that you see?

- How are they building from one day's experience to the next?
- What new ideas, solutions, or answers are the children coming up with? Is there a way to build on these?

Step 3: Enrich the play

If you notice interest waning or the children needing more complexity to sustain their involvement, enrich the project with props that might add new ideas. For instance in the "Caring for Babies" project you might:

- introduce doctor kits or books about the growth and development of babies;
- arrange for the children to bring in their baby pictures and develop a guessing game or display with them;
- have a visit from a real baby or take a field trip to a hospital nursery;
- explore where babies come from and how they grow and come into the world; or
- include examples of different kinds of animal babies, perhaps leading to classifications of how babies are born in different animal families— mammals, birds, reptiles, and so forth.

Step 4: Represent the experience

The last step in the process is to collect and display documentation of the children's thinking and evolution of the project. These questions will help you consider how to represent what happened:

- What were their beginning ideas and actions?
- What occurred after they worked with the theme over time?
- How have the children's ideas and actions changed?

- How can you summarize what they learned?
- What questions, interests and needs emerged that may lead to a new theme?

Children's Representations. An important role for you as a teacher is to help children represent their thinking and experiences. As they do this, they develop "the hundred languages" referred to in the schools of Reggio Emelia. Children expand their symbolic thinking, creative expression, and visual literacy. Representation, or using symbols to represent ideas, is the foundation for broader language and literacy development.

During the "Caring for Babies" project, you could ask children to try using blocks to create a nursery like the one they saw in their field trip to the hospital. Children can represent their ideas working with clay, drawings, and dictated stories.

Teacher Representation. It is valuable for teachers to make representations of the children's ideas as well. You can write down their words and read them back or take photos and caption them together. Telling stories or creating finger plays about the children's activities are other representations.

Teachers can sketch child creations such as a block structure, make photocopies, and post one near the block area, or put copies on the art table the next day. Children love the recognition they get when teachers represent what they have been doing. It gives further impetus for their own representations. Representing and re-representing deepens understandings and the collaborative learning process. (See *Spreading the News* listed in the Recommended Resources section for more detailed ideas on teacher representation.)

Practice the Planning Process

With the four steps just described, practice this planning process with these examples of teacher observations.

Initial provision of the environment.

Things to sustain the play.

Ways to enrich the theme.

Options for children to represent the experience.

The teacher notices children repeatedly pretending to talk on the phone. Fill in your ideas for enriching and building on this theme using the four steps.

The teacher hears the children's excitement about a fire they saw on the news. Plan a curriculum using the four steps.

Initial provision of the environment.

Things to sustain the play.

Ways to enrich the theme.

Options for children to represent the experience.

Representing the Curriculum to Others

Most people use school as their frame of reference for planning curriculum. Supervisors, parents, and regulatory agencies expect to see a school-type lesson plan form posted in your room. They think this indicates that you are teaching children what they need to know before entering school.

Because the approach to child-centered curriculum planning advocated in this handbook uses childhood, not school, as a reference point, curriculum plans cannot be confined to little boxes representing times and days of the week. This means you will have to re-educate others about what to expect. They need help in understanding how what you are doing meets the intent of the requirements or expectations they have.

There are a variety of strategies you can use to meet desires or requirements for written curriculum plans. You'll find examples here you can copy or adapt to meet your specific needs. Experiment with them until you find a format that works for you and satisfies the expectations of others.

Post your pre-thinking about a curriculum project using the form on the next page. If you are required to use a preschool planning form, translate the ideas of "provision-sustain-enrich-represent" into their boxes. You can continue to use this form for yourself to document what actually happens as the curriculum evolves.

137

Curriculum Plans for _____

Project Theme: _____

Initial provision of the environment.

Things to sustain the play.

Ways to enrich the theme.

Options for children to represent the experience.

Color-Coded Web

Use a curriculum web format to document the curriculum process as it emerges. You can use one color to indicate interests and responses on the part of the children and another color to describe teacher provisions, interventions, enrichments, and so forth. The following web is an example of a form for documenting the curriculum process as it emerges.

Example:
Teacher reads *Welcoming Babies.*

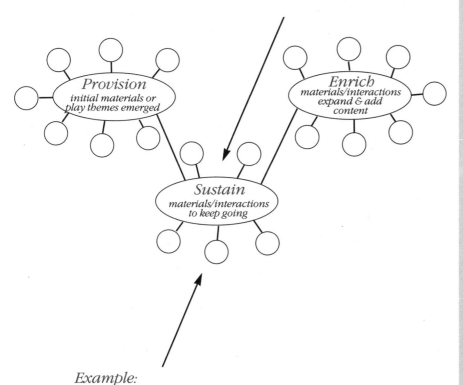

Example:
Diane brought pictures of herself as a baby.

Stages-of-Play Web

Plan your environment and activities for any topic or project around the four stages of play. A possible form for this is included here. In creating your own web, start with your starting place, provocation, or topical theme in the center of the page.

Sensory and Exploratory Play

Environment/ Materials:

Activities:

Requirements met:

Building and Constructive Play

Environment/ Materials:

Activities:

Requirements met:

Possible theme or provocation

Roles and Symbolic Play

Environment/ Materials:

Activities:

Requirements met:

Games and Rules

Environment/ Materials:

Activities:

Requirements met:

Webbing from Topical to Developmental Themes

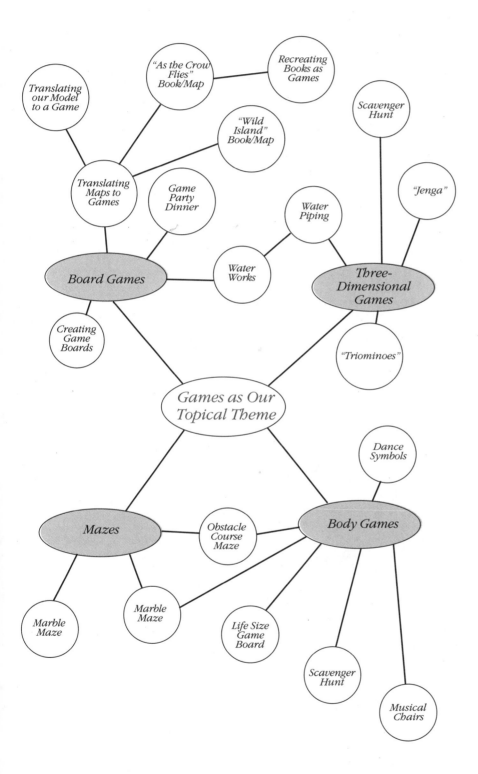

Use a web format to compare how a topical theme in your curriculum uncovered the developmental themes of children. Sample webs are included below.

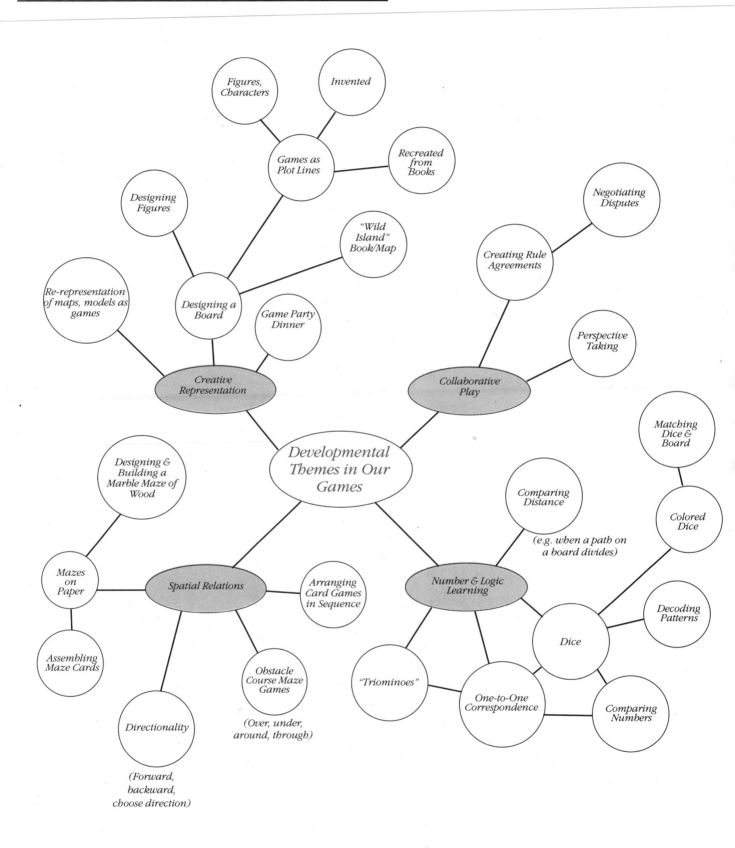

Portfolios and Documentation Displays

- Create individual child portfolios and large bulletin board displays with photographs, quotes, and work samples from children that show the development of their interests, questions, and learning process. Many examples of this are included in our earlier book, *Spreading the News: Sharing the Stories of Early Childhood Programs* and *The Portfolio and Its Use* (see the Recommended Resources section).

Practice Becoming Articulate
About Your Curriculum Approach

At some point, you will probably have to represent your curriculum to others in conversations or presentations. Use the following activities to develop yourself as a spokesperson and guardian of childhood.

1. I can't tell if my child is learning anything in your class if she doesn't bring home art projects every day.

2. If you don't plan an activity for each part of the day, won't the kids just get bored with free play?

3. What if my child just wants to play with blocks all day and not learn anything?

4. Are you going to teach my child to read in this class?

Practice responding to these questions to sharpen your skills at describing how your curriculum is meeting children's needs and parent concerns.

Work alone or in a small group with teachers to develop an initial letter to parents regarding your approach to curriculum planning.

Sometimes you must communicate with parents in writing. Use this activity to develop your collaborative writing skills on how you plan curriculum. Create a letter to parents of more than one page. Because group writing can be difficult, you might want to use the following process:

1. Brainstorm a list of points to include.

2. Decide on priorities, grouping related points together.

3. Number the order in which you wish to cover the points

4. Write a paragraph for each set of points.

5. Write your final copy.

About Your Planning

and

Communication

Use this space to make notes about how you communicate your planning approach. These questions will get you started.

What would you like to learn to communicate about your approach to curriculum planning?

What specific topics and skills do you want to focus on?

A Whale of a Good Time:
A Story About Using
Multiple Intelligences

Connie Gassner,
Kindergarten Teacher

The following is a story from my teaching journey. It is a story of learning to pay attention to the children, supporting their interests, and letting go of my agenda. It involves a field trip that came at the beginning of a curriculum plan and took the children and me beyond our initial inquiry process in ways that far surpassed my expectations. The experience was very gratifying not only for the children, but for me as well. It shed new light on what is possible when we follow the children's lead.

After involvement in the "Taking Care of Animals" program of the Indianapolis, Indiana, Zoo, my plan was to have our child care center kindergarten class list favorite zoo animals and vote on one animal to discuss each day. We began with the inquiry process I had learned to use and listed what we knew, what we wanted to know, and what we had learned.

During our morning group time, the class chose an animal to research. I said that anyone interested in that particular animal could use the learning center time to explore answers to our inquiry list. The children's research involved exploring animal books, magazines, and encyclopedias. At the end of the day, we met and reviewed what we now knew about the questions of the morning. This continued for a few days with a few different animals being explored; we also learned zoo songs and finger plays and read zoo stories.

One morning Steve mentioned that his favorite animal was the whale and he wished we could learn more about it. Actually, I had hoped that my favorite

These three stories are from three very large institutions with enclaves of teachers and coordinators on the road to making changes toward a more child-centered approach with their curriculum.

animal, the hippo, would be the choice of that day. But to my chagrin, Steve's interest won over the children and whales became the focus. We used the same inquiry process to start with, but the list of questions went beyond any other animal information we had already explored.

Many children helped with the research on whales that day. The information we discovered led us to more and more questions. By our closing group time, some of the children and I promised to check at home for whale information so we could continue the next day.

Our whale enthusiasm led us to an ocean of whale research and learning. I became as excited as the children and searched for whale information and materials. Colleagues came to my rescue with materials, including a whale puppet, story books, games, and posters. Sarah and I brought postcards from Sea World, and Bryce brought his mammal book from home. I introduced Whales, the Big Book Magazine, and we were off to a most exciting adventure.

There were so many discoveries during this curriculum that I practiced categorizing the activities using Howard Gardner's theory of multiple intelligences as my own assessment of how this curriculum reached the different interests and learning styles of my kindergartners. Following is a summary of what this included.

Linguistic: We used the whale puppet to read stories and plays, including *Ibus: A True Story* by John Himmelman, Raffi's *Baby Beluga*, the Big Book Magazine *Whales*, and the plays *Humphrey, the Wrong-Way Whale* and *The Magic Pail.* The last was a story of a whale granting a fisherman a pail with three wishes in return for his freedom. We drew or wrote our own three wishes on pail-shaped paper. Children also had the opportunity to write whale stories in whale-shaped blank writing books. There was constant discussion about our questions and what we were learning about whales.

Logical/Mathematical: We graphed and classified the baleen and toothed whales. The children also compared the sizes of the different whales. We discovered the blue whale is the size of three buses, the right whale is two buses, and the beluga is one car length. We learned the weights and lengths of the different whales. We read the poem "A Thought," which compared the size of a whale to a snail (big and small). We compared fish and whales and learned that whales are mammals, hot-blooded like humans. They have lungs and need to come up for air. Some large whales can stay under water for one hour.

Spatial: We hung whale posters on the classroom walls and had a whale big book available. Whale information was written on charts. Whale stencils of different sizes were drawn and cut. Whale postcards were mounted on posters. A map of the U.S. West Coast was enlarged, and we routed the migration of the whales between Mexico (where the young are born) and Alaska. I shared a personal story of my adventure as a teacher in California when a group of our students went whale-watching on a class trip. The Pacific Ocean was very choppy that day, causing most of the students to become seasick. But the students did have the opportunity to see a mother and baby bobbing in and out of the water together.

Bodily/Kinesthetic: Children made 3-D whales by stuffing cotton into stapled whale-shaped construction paper. Some created mother and baby whales together which I hung from the ceiling. Others painted a huge whale on a large piece of paper taped to the floor. They decided to use blue, black, white, and gray (which they discovered as they mixed the black and white paint together). The painting of this whale was an amazing process. The first group painted the entire whale blue. Then others added their special touches: a little white, a dab of gray, black on the tail. Someone even added a blow hole with the water and air spouting out. The children continued to add individual touches as they passed by the large whale in process during the day. The end result was as magnificent as the process. It is now hanging in the hallway for everyone to admire.

Musical: We danced and sang to "Baby Beluga" by Raffi and listened to whale sounds on the Song of the Whales cassette during rest time. The idea of whales singing in and of itself offers insights into musical intelligence!

Interpersonal: The children found whale books from the book mobile and groups gathered together to discuss the pictures. One book had photos of people hunting whales, which led us to discussions and debates of the probability of endangered whales. The children asked why people kill whales and we learned that people use these animals for food, oil, and skins. Some children felt that whales should be protected and together planned how they would go about doing this.

Intrapersonal: Children used their private journals to write or draw about whales. Some children seemed to enjoy listening to the whale tape in the listening center using the earphones. They also sat on pillows in the quiet areas, enthralled in the whale books, seemingly lost in thought for long periods of time.

A curriculum project like this finds its own way to wind down. It was time to bring it to a close as we noticed we were becoming "whaled out." While we may never get to study the hippo, that seems frivolous to me now. What we might have learned by trying to cover all the other zoo animals as part of my curriculum could not compare to our excitement in learning about whales. I think the children got a taste of pursuing a passion to gather information and learn—something that will influence their lives to come.

As a teacher, this experience taught me that learning becomes relevant and important for children when adults allow them to make choices from their interests and support them in gathering their own information. In this curriculum, we all became an active part of a meaningful learning process. To me, this is what emergent curriculum is all about. It's the kind of teaching that keeps me going.

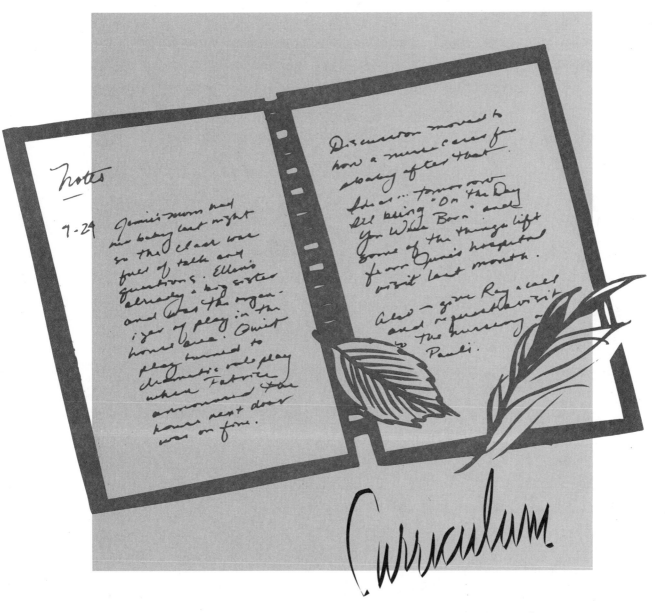

Curriculum
is Just One Big Spider Web:
A Dialogue About Changing Our Head Start Classrooms

Toni Washington, Head Teacher,
and Frances Jones Baker, Education Coordinator

uring the last few years, our Head Start program has made some important shifts in how we approach curriculum. The process has been a slow one, and involved changing our curriculum model, offering trainings, and giving each teacher a chance to find her or his own way to make the necessary changes.

The following is our reflection on the process, including where we were and how things are opening up now to better meet the needs of the children.

FJB: Our approach to curriculum in the past felt robotic to me. Everybody was doing the same thing. There wasn't room for any creativity. We had a really creative group that was being stifled. Teachers felt like they couldn't bring their real selves into the classroom and make it exciting. Everybody was kind of just going through the motions. They were doing things that really weren't exciting for them.

TW: We were doing the curriculum, following the program guidelines.

FJB: Right. Everybody was doing the same theme, at the same time, same month. When we first talked about using a different curriculum model, the teachers were wary of the changes we were suggesting and wondered how this would be different. But then they realized that we were providing a framework and they could do with it what they wanted within that framework—then they really took off.

Now I can enter each classroom and everything looks totally different. In the past, the rooms were set up exactly the same. Now, you see some great room arrangements, some of them very unique.

TW: Our teachers have started to address the children versus a curriculum. We are no longer recycling the same things year after year. The room environment doesn't stay the same from year to year and neither do the bulletin boards. That's a big change. Now we are addressing who these children are, this group, these families, this year.

Now, I always tell kids, " This is our room. All the responsibilities are ours to clean up, to decorate." They bring in pictures of their family to post in the classroom immediately.

FJB: When children think of the room as theirs, you see cleanup and maintenance happen so much smoother. When children don't buy into what's there, in terms of activities and materials, it's like pulling teeth to get them to clean up. When you go into some of these classrooms now you can tell they feel it is their space. They know the routines and care about them so much that they can become teachers when someone is out. They are really helpful to the substitutes.

TW: We even have the children answering the phone now. This started with some children who had speech needs, but then we needed to involve everyone. This is their home away from home and answering the phone is one way to show it. You have to trust your kids, respect them. They will show you that respect in return.

It's really about following the lead of the child. And most of the time the ones you are following are the ones who need nurturing. So that's why I always tell parents, "You know, it's okay for your child to bring something from home. I want them to be able to share, to talk about the object and explain where they got it, what it means to them, and so on." It just brings those kids out. And then when I follow the lead from that child, do you know what that does for that child, and his self-esteem? It has made a huge difference for the children and for us to do curriculum this way.

A little boy named Eric brought in a remote control car in his backpack. Perfect. It's time to do a transportation curriculum. Let's give the parents a call and ask, "What do you have at home that will help us learn about transportation?" It involves the parents this way. The whole family. We have a father who is a bus driver who can come in and bring the bus.

Now we are going to learn all about transportation—things on the land and sea, air. We'll count how many tires and engines. It's just going to open up whole new avenues. Just walking on field trips, seeing how people get back and forth to school, how people carry their children on their backs as a form of transportation. So we'll get into a cultural thing. It just opens it up—all from a child bringing a remote control car to school. To me that's following that child's lead. And those are themes you already have in the back of your mind that you want to do anyway.

FJB: I think the change in our scheduling too has made a difference. It allows a bulk of time for children to have a work time and teachers feed into their interests and can really get involved in their play more extensively than in the past when it was chopped up in little blocks of time. Children have more time to talk about what they are doing as they do it and teachers hear what they are talking about and what they are developing in the block area or in the quiet area.

TW: And take pictures and acknowledge what they have done. You really have to get down to their level. Before, my job was to teach them lessons, set up the house area, set up this and that, and observe what they did and write it down. We were asked, "Do you have documentation?"

The questions for me became: What are we doing with all this documentation? What are we doing with what the children are saying and what their interests are? Can we build on their play?

For example, in the home center when you hear a child say, "I want to go to California," can you be there and hear that? Can you allow a little bit more interaction to go on and see what the kids are going to say to one another while you are watching? You do some quick thinking and then you can slide on in there. "I heard you say you want to go to California. How can you get there? Do others want to come with us? Maybe you can involve those in the block area if they need more help. Maybe we can go over here and take a bus. 'Hey you guys, we need a bus. Can you get us a bus ready so we can get to California?' We need tickets. Maybe we can go over to the art area and see if there are some kids cutting and we can ask them, 'Hey, can you make us some tickets to get on our bus?' We may need to go to the quiet area to pick up something else."

Your observation recognizes the curriculum that is actually happening and it may not have anything to do with what's written on your lesson plan. So let's turn the page and start over. You can go back to something else you have already planned and extend it. We already have a lot of resources right here because we may have already dealt with this theme before. We can extend from that and not keep writing new things over and over.

FJB: Sometimes when I'm in these classrooms and see so much going on I forget to ask to see the lesson plans. Yes, you do have to have lesson plans so I know you are thinking ahead. But I'm not going to hold teachers to that if I see the children are involved and their needs are being met. To me, that's more important than what's on the paper.

That's why I think it's real important that we just step back sometimes and reassess. We have a lot of paperwork and we can get so caught up, that we forget why we're doing what we're doing. Sometimes lesson plans and other documentation may not be where it's supposed to be, but are the children getting what they need to be getting in the classroom? To me, that's the key. We can keep working on the other things.

This year we reorganized the lesson plan book and moved the page about individualizing for children to the front of each week. Your plan is focusing on these six kids that week and how you are meeting their needs, not on a general curriculum plan itself. This gives you tremendous flexibility as you are focusing on specific kids.

TW: I tell my assistant teacher as she learns to plan, "Go ahead and do a lesson plan because you need to be prepared. But if the flow doesn't go that way and it just didn't happen that way, then come back to it another time." Believe you me, you will be able to spider web that theme later on because that's all that curriculum is—just one big spider web.

This has been a natural change for me. It was me all along. It has to be part of you. You have to teach from who you are. What brought you to this job anyway? What excites you about working with children? You must open up and bring some of your creativity and pay attention to the creativity of the children. Let it work both ways.

FJB: When the teachers are real, the children are real. They know that there are a variety of personalities and this teacher is one. It amazes me that they feel free to say what they want to say and not be nervous. They know they will be respected. What they say gets incorporated into a little lesson. They feel free to be themselves and they learn from it.

TW: Isn't that what Head Start is all about, giving them a head start? We are supposed to be about preparing the children to live in society, not just getting ready for kindergarten. Oh, they're going to get those school lessons when they get there. But that's not all we're about. We need to address who they are as a person so that they can be successful when they get to kindergarten. Academics are important, yes, I validate that. But that's not the whole picture.

Yesterday I brought the record player down to the gym to use music for a movement activity that needed more space. We could turn it up as loud as we wanted to. The music sounded so good and we enjoyed it so much that we just left it on for the rest of free play time. Pretty soon the song we use to signal it's time for cleanup came on and the children went right into their routine of cleaning up. So I just said to myself, "There are so many ways to do this thing. Let's just have fun. I'll just play from their lead."

They were so into the music, having such a good time, I didn't want to turn it off. I asked myself, "Now does it make sense for me to go back in the classroom and sing this same song again because it's on the lesson plan for this time?" They were riding trikes and tumbling and singing our circle time together. Then when the cleanup song came on, it pulled them back together. They were in tune when they heard it. They started cleaning up, putting things away, and heading for the door. I didn't have to announce cleanup. We were just singing, cleaning up, lining up. We did numbers, counting tricycles as we put them away. We sang hello to one another. We did all the things we might do in circle time, but we were in the gym, up and moving. Like I said, "Curriculum is just one big spider web."

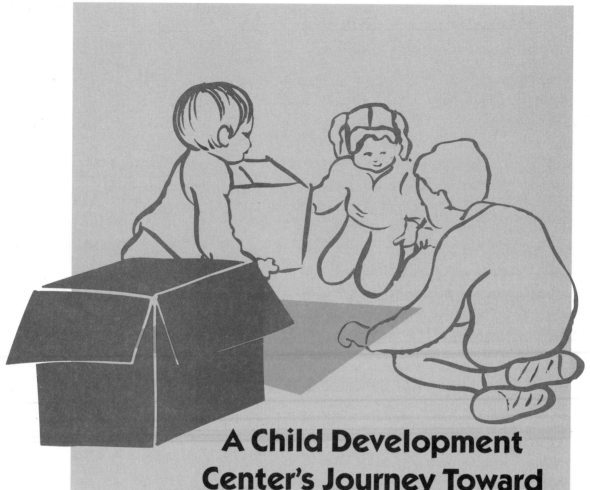

A Child Development Center's Journey Toward Emergent Curriculum:

An Administrator's Story

Barbara McPherson,
Training and Curriculum Specialist

I n the corporate world, business and industry are realigning. They are trying to empower their employees, the little people, to increase productivity, solve problems, and increase job satisfaction. The new buzz words are "total quality management." Historically, business procedures and practices have usually come from the top down, and the child care industry has not been exempt from this practice. Regulations, policies, standing operating procedures, program design, and even curriculum are usually dispensed from the top down. The following is a story about a large child care organization and how it successfully realigned its curriculum process and discovered total quality management from a surprising source—the children.

Our setting

The setting for this story is a child development center located at Fort Lewis, Washington, one of the many programs provided for military families through Child Development Services in the Department of the Army. At Fort Lewis we care for children ages six weeks to twelve years of age. Our center offers a variety of child care programs, including full-day and part-day preschool, hourly care, and school-age care. Of the approximately one hundred staff members employed, forty are infant and toddler teachers, forty work as preschool and school-age teachers, and twenty are support staff, including administrators. As the trainer for the preschool and school-age staff, my responsibility is to monitor developmental programming and facilitate the professional development of staff, which includes providing training on how to develop curriculum and write and implement lesson plans.

Our curriculum story

In the past, the center administrators, including the center director, assistant director, and the training and curriculum specialists, have developed program curriculum. The administrators gave the curriculum to the classroom teachers along with a monthly calendar of the themes, special events, and lesson plans. The classroom teachers presented this curriculum to their children.

Most themes and concepts were explored for a week, but some were only scheduled for a day. Teachers struggled to quickly change the environment and stock the learning centers with hands-on materials so that the children could play and absorb the theme. Many of the themes tended to result in teacher-directed activities, limiting children's choices.

Teachers became quickly exhausted. They couldn't physically gather materials and change the environment fast enough. The children often weren't involved in a theme long enough to explore it with meaning. In short, the people who knew the children best—the teachers—were not planning the curriculum.

A plan for change

I began lobbying for ownership of the curriculum in order to get it into the teachers' hands. At first, these efforts were only marginally successful. The teachers wrote their own lesson plans using predetermined themes that changed every week from top-fed curriculum sources. A year passed.

The director recognized the teachers' enthusiasm and the creativity that was being generated by their freedom to choose activities. We then moved forward another step. The teachers, as a group, could now choose the curriculum themes that the center would teach. Each month they met to select themes, compile curriculum resources, and develop their lesson plans. Wow! We thought we were so developmentally appropriate. Teachers were selecting themes that they and the children enjoyed. Two years passed.

A new idea

One day I went to volunteer in my son's first grade classroom. As I was correcting papers, his teacher began a strange activity. She wrote the word elephant on the blackboard and drew a circle around it. The teacher then told the children they were going to "web" elephant. Obviously, the children knew what she meant because they began to describe an elephant. They called out comments about what elephants looked like, what they ate, and where they lived. The teacher kept putting the children's words in circles and connecting them with lines.

The web started to grow and I saw its purpose. The teacher was connecting the children's ideas and creating a learning path. The web, filled with potential curriculum possibilities, was generated from the children. I went back to our child development center recharged.

My new goal was to include children in the curriculum process. That would be easy, right? I would just waltz into the center and say, "Hey, everybody, let's have the kids create the curriculum, okay?" Although I didn't say that, I talked with the teachers about curriculum. I asked them what was and wasn't working for them and the children.

Their response was, "It's hard to change the theme every two weeks. Just when we get the learning centers filled with materials that reflect the theme, the theme changes. The kids don't have enough time to fully explore the topic." We discovered that though the teachers now owned the curriculum, the outcomes had not really changed.

At the next staff meeting I shared my webbing experience and broached the idea with the teachers. They weren't sure what I was talking about, and neither was I. However, they humored me and at the next meeting we began to web. The teachers chose the beach as a theme and webbed it. What do you find at the beach? What do you do at the beach? We called this a concept web and each web provided curriculum for a month. The teachers had the freedom to pick and choose what parts of the web they wanted to concentrate on depending on their children's needs. Another year went by.

Getting closer to the source

Throughout the year I role-modeled how to web with school-aged children. Teachers were reluctant. A colleague from the local community college kept telling me that I should read the book *Emergent Curriculum* by Elizabeth Jones and John Nimmo (NAEYC, 1995). This book gave me a foundation to build upon.

The next step was to have each classroom create a web for themselves. We have achieved this goal. Each of our classrooms now has a different web for anywhere from two weeks to a month, depending on the children's interests and the teachers' interests. The teachers have been empowered. They have become the decision-makers who are valued for their knowledge about the children.

Six months passed before I discovered the draft of *Reflecting Children's Lives* by Deb Curtis and Margie Carter. The text became an excellent resource and provided me with information on how to train teachers in emergent curriculum. The next step was to include children in the webbing process, especially school-agers.

I developed a training, incorporating handouts from *Reflecting Children's Lives,* and trained teachers on components of emergent curriculum. We specifically focused on provisioning, sustaining, enriching, and representing children's learning experiences. The final step for the teachers and for me was realizing that observation was the key to the whole process of emergent curriculum. What were the children playing? What concepts were the children exploring and how could we scaffold their learning? Children generate the curriculum in each classroom now and teachers facilitate their learning process!

What are the results? Teachers are enthusiastic and that has increased productivity. The teachers' attention is focused on the children. That, in turn, reinforces the teachers' knowledge of child development as they deduce what concepts the children are exploring. The amount of literacy that has surfaced during the representation stage is staggering. Parents are overjoyed. Children have been empowered. School-aged children especially have become vested in their learning process and are verbalizing their needs.

Yesterday a kindergartner said to me, "Teacher Barb, we need to go to the post office. Can we go on a field trip?" I asked him why his class needed to go to the post office. He replied, "We're going to make dramatic play into a post office and we want to see a real one to see what they got." Now, that's total quality management from the bottom up!

Developing Yourself

A child-centered,

emergent approach to

curriculum

is a lifestyle —

a set of beliefs

and values

that influence teaching

behaviors.

7

Think of a time when you had to make a significant change in your life and you were successful. Remember the details of what that success was like—remember the feelings, sounds, and people involved.

- **What kept you motivated to stay on track?**
- **Were there mentors or role models that you looked to?**
- **How did you get through times of stress and discouragement?**
- **What kept you learning and growing?**

A Journey of

Personal and Professional

Development

A child-centered, emergent approach to curriculum isn't just a method or teaching technique. It is a lifestyle—a set of beliefs and values that influence teaching behaviors. This approach requires a complex set of skills and knowledge and, most importantly, particular attitudes and dispositions.

You probably spent your school years as a student in teacher-directed, content-focused classrooms. Your own experience of education is usually contrary to what you want to be doing with children. Using a child-centered approach requires that you recreate a new vision of education.

Whether you work as a home provider or center-based caregiver, you must reinvent the role of the teacher. You must begin to trust yourself, and the children you work with, to keep growing and learning. And you must be willing to go up against the status quo, to challenge and advocate for meaningful learning environments for yourself and the children.

New Roles

for Providers and Teachers

Most people enter the child care field with ideas about the role they can play in children's learning. They want to pass along knowledge, shape children's minds, do fun crafts, and get children ready for school and future jobs. With this in mind, they tend to use the only model they are familiar with—school. They water down the activities in an attempt to make them developmentally appropriate.

But at this point in our country's history, childhood is under assault and has been seriously eroded. Children need you to provide something much more profound than lessons on colors and holiday crafts.

Today, the real needs of children in our program include:

- Real time to pursue curiosity, interests, skills
- Real work, not meaningless tasks or projects
- Real things to develop their bodies, not subdue them
- Real guidance, not punishment
- Real role models, not superheroes or celebrities
- Real reflections of their lives, not commercial or cartoon renditions.

Teachers who are truly providing a child-centered curriculum are playing different roles than the typical ones of cheerleader, disciplinarian, and timekeeper. Planning curriculum along the lines described in this handbook requires a new way of thinking about adult roles and behaviors.

Try thinking of yourself in some new ways. How is what you do like the work of an archeologist, forecaster, advocate, improvisational artist, or scientist? Make a list of the skills and responsibilities of these roles and see how they compare with yours. The better you get at articulating what you do, the more effective you become in securing the respect and compensation that comes with these jobs. Consider the "Teacher As…" examples on the following pages.

167

Teacher as Architect

- Evaluating space based on a child's eye view
- Adapting space to the children's play needs and interests
- Creating opportunities to explore light and shadow, sound, color and texture
- Integrating outdoor and natural world elements into the indoor environment
- Rearranging the environment to create new interest in each area

Teacher as Observer

- Seeing self as a field researcher in child development
- Appreciating the details of children's complex play
- Making note of a child's likes, dislikes, accomplishments and frustrations
- Observing before intervening or reacting
- Planning curriculum projects from children's interests and ideas

Teacher as Prop Manager

- Suggesting play possibilities through arrangement of materials
- Anticipating playscripts with a supply of related props
- Encouraging open-ended use and transformation of materials
- Creating order behind the play with casual picking up and putting away
- Providing additional materials without interrupting the play flow

Teacher as Mediator

- Creating a climate of safety for children to speak their needs and feelings
- Seeing conflicts as opportunities to learn social skills

- Providing support and language for children to solve their own problems
- Focusing on the content of the play rather than on a violation of rules
- Interpreting the meaning of children's messages to each other

Teacher as Coach

- Recognizing strengths and providing opportunities to practice them
- Encouraging risk-taking with a supportive presence
- Teaching skills to support self-selected tasks
- Matching challenges to individual interests
- Creating teamwork with materials and activities that require group effort

Teacher as Scribe

- Modeling that the spoken word can be written down and read
- Making written and pictorial representations of children's play and language
- Telling stories to children about their own play activities
- Taking dictation or transcribing children's language
- Supporting children's efforts to tell stories or write about their play or creations

Teacher as Broadcaster

- Spreading the news of the play stories you observe in your group
- Collecting and displaying examples of children's activities and creations
- Representing a child's point of view about a significant event
- Sharing children's good ideas with others
- Educating parents about the learning embedded in their child's chosen play

Self-Assessment

What behaviors are part of your daily caregiving and teaching? Use the following checklist to assess yourself and then set goals for new knowledge and skills you want to acquire. Seek out workshops and classes; find a mentor- someone who can serve as a model, coach, and peer consultant for you. If you have checked most of the items below, consider becoming a mentor for someone else.

☐ I am providing additional props to keep play going.

☐ I am mediating conflict to promote continuous self-initiated play.

☐ I am allowing messes when related to productive play.

☐ I am maintaining order behind the scenes to keep the play going.

☐ I am avoiding interventions that sidetrack children's play themes.

☐ I am telling stories using children's play themes during group times.

☐ I am incorporating children's themes into curriculum planning and community building.

☐ I am enthusiastically documenting, representing, and discussing children's play with co-workers and parents.

☐ I am being playful in interactions and sharing my own interests with children.

☐ I am regularly collaborating with my co-workers.

Cultivating your Dispositions

Master teachers in child-centered programs have certain qualities that distinguish them from teachers who depend on curriculum activity books, follow the same theme plans year after year, or struggle daily to get the children involved in anything productive. The knowledge and skill of master teachers is not necessarily different from other teachers. Rather, these professionals have a set of attitudes and habits of mind that enable them to respond to the classroom dynamics and multiple needs of children with the readiness of an improvisational artist.

Lilian Katz refers to these habits of mind or tendencies to respond to certain situations in certain ways as dispositions. Curiosity, friendliness or unfriendliness, bossiness, and creativity are dispositions, or sets of dispositions, rather than skills or a kind of knowledge.

Explore this idea of dispositions by completing the "Dispositions for Child-Centered Programs" form on page 172. First, think about yourself or a specific teacher with whom you work. Get a clear picture in your mind of typical facial and verbal expressions and body language. Where do you usually find yourself or this teacher in the classroom? Then, with a pen or pencil, mark where you think you or this teacher falls on each of the seven lines of disposition continuums.

Cultivate these dispositions in yourself, and you will find that creating child-centered programs and curriculum will come more naturally.

A disposition is a "prevailing tendency, mood, or inclination; a temperamental makeup; and the tendency to act in a certain manner under given circumstances."

— *Webster's New Collegiate Dictionary*

Mark where you fall on each line of these "disposition continuums." Discover your attitudes and habits of mind.

What changes would you like to see?

Dispositions for Child-Centered Programs

Has a mindset about chidren that reveals curiosity & delight in who they are & what they do.	Seems to like kids but can't tell you why.	Approaches children primarily to correct them or direct them in an activity.
Values play, plans for it in setting up the environment, & watches closely to see what the children do.	Lets play happen in the classroom so as to have time to tend to other teacher chores.	Views free play as time for children to "blow off steam" in between teacher-directed activities.
Expects children to change & challenge plans and remains flexible to follow their interests & questions.	Allows children to briefly digress from planned activities, but then gets them back on task.	Is highly invested in having teacher-planned activities carried out by the children.
Is willing to try new things & take risks for the benefit of the children's & her or his own learning as a teacher.	Seldom initiates anything with children outside of tried and true activities.	Has his or her own way of doing things and resists new ways and ideas.

Continually examines experiences & her or his own actions in search of new understandings.	Rolls with the punches and doesn't think much more about it.	Doesn't see own role or impact on classroom events; tends to see others as the cause of things not going well.
Alert and active in addressing a bias or the limitations of the status quo.	May agree when a bias is pointed out or a change is called for, but is reluctant to speak or upset anyone.	Doesn't notice and thus participates in perpetuating bias and the limitations of the status quo.
Actively seeks collaboration and believes two heads are better than one.	Is pleased when asked to join in, but it doesn't occur to him or her to seek out collaboration.	Has his or her own way of doing things and prefers to work alone.

Useful

Dispositions to Acquire

Delight in and be curious about children's development

Most providers and teachers enjoy children and their learning process. This enjoyment is a primary motivation for taking on the work of teaching young children. Once on the job, however, with the pressures of trying to conduct activities, manage behaviors, and maintain order in the classroom, teachers commonly lose that sense of delight. They soon become more focused on the goals of their curriculum plans rather than on the learning process of children. Typically, teachers jump to control misbehavior, rather than ponder the reasons for a child's actions. Delight and curiosity come easily when you truly watch children. Curiosity leads to more job satisfaction as well.

Value children's play

Play is of value in and of itself, but adults easily lose track of this fact. Children who are independently involved in play often go unnoticed by teachers, who use this time for other pressing needs in their job (such as record-keeping, housekeeping, resource gathering and filing, or consulting with a co-worker, parent, or supervisor).

Teachers who value play recognize that the best curriculum emerges out of the themes children are investigating and expressing, rather than from a commercial activity book or file of last year's plans.

Cultivate these

dispositions

in yourself,

and you will find

that creating

child-centered

programs

and curriculum

will come

more naturally.

When teachers can identify the kinds of play occurring in their classrooms, they deepen their understandings of child development and get better at planning for individual children.

Expect continuous change and challenge

The nature of early childhood involves intense change and challenge. This is the context for the daily work of teachers, requiring them to make continuous on-the-spot decisions and judgment calls. Teachers respond more effectively when they expect constant changes and challenges and make them central to their work.

Be willing to take risks and make mistakes

As you come to expect continuous change and challenge, a willingness to take risks and make mistakes naturally follows. Without this you won't grow. Children need to see this disposition modeled so they too will be willing to try and not have their self-esteem or self-confidence undermined by making mistakes.

Provide time for regular reflection and self-examination

People learn from reflecting on experience and from analyzing events, dynamics, and conclusions. You also learn from comparing the "official word" or theory with your own intuition and experience. Reflection may confirm or contradict previous understandings. Either way, it deepens insights and the disposition toward seeing yourself as a lifelong learner.

Teachers not predisposed to self-reflection and evaluation tend to attribute all classroom difficulties to someone else: It's the children who are too immature, disrespectful, or out of control. Even if that's true, this is only half of the story. You need to gain perspectives on how your behaviors, expectations, and patterns from your own childhood experience impact the situations you set up for children.

Seek collaboration and peer support

Though working with children can be delightful, it can also be isolating. Regular discussion with peers helps you sustain your self-reflection process and learn the value of different approaches. These conversations can involve getting feedback on ideas, sharing teaching strategies, and gaining support. Joining with colleagues, you can make changes in yourself and in your working conditions, compensation, and the quality of care and education for children.

Be a professional watchdog and a whistle blower

Providers and classroom teachers are under tremendous pressure to meet other people's needs. It is not only children who present you with numerous demands, but also parents, supervisors, and assessments for school readiness. Without a solid footing in the developmental theory and appropriate practices of child-centered curriculum, you can easily slip into accepting a "pushdown" academic curriculum.

You need to embolden yourself to become advocates for childhood and for your own needs as a teacher. You need to speak up when decisions, policies, and the media are headed down the wrong path.

Practice

Identifying Dispositions

A home provider, Naomi, and her assistant, Sandria, are supervising children on the playground. Three four-year-old children are playing together on the climber. They are using a rope to lift a metal bucket full of sand to the top of the climber platform.

Sandria tells Naomi, "I've told those kids to stop using the bucket that way. I think it's too dangerous."

"I feel a bit nervous about how safe that is too," Naomi responds, "but let's watch what they do for a moment before we stop them."

"Look how they figured out how to tie the rope to the bucket and then around the climber," says Sandria. "They've invented a complex system, almost like a pulley."

"And look how much cooperation it's taking to get the bucket to the top without spilling the sand. This activity seems too valuable to stop," Naomi observes. "What can we do to make it safer?"

Sandria replies, "Maybe we can exchange the metal bucket for a plastic one, so the danger will be less."

Rather than quickly reacting to and stopping the children's play, these providers are taking time to observe, reflect, and analyze the value of what is happening. Sandria and Naomi are conscientious about safety concerns, but weigh the risks in light of the value of these children's investigation and

Read through the following scenario and look for the dispositions these people display.

A Closer Look

cooperative play. They collaborate and find a solution, allowing for an acceptable risk in order for the children's learning to continue.

A Commitment to

 *Ongoing* **Self-Evaluation and Growth**

Before you can really implement a child-centered approach, you must examine your own attitudes and experiences and take steps to rid your curriculum of meaningless activities and tired ideas. Children need teachers who are passionate, curious, joyful, and committed to living life fully mindful. Following are some ideas to cultivate these qualities in yourself.

Learning from Children

Careful observations remind us that children approach the world with a fresh and open attitude. Children explore with wonder and excitement because they are experiencing things for the first time. They haven't yet accommodated themselves to adult confines, discouragement, deadened senses, or lowered self-esteem and confidence. Reclaim your own wonder by learning from children involved in activities like the following.

Sam, 10 months old, intently grabs at his shadow made by the sun streaming through the window above him. Then he puts his face down and touches the shadow with his tongue and lips.

Amber, a toddler, puts her whole body into the sensory table filled with macaroni. She moves back and forth through the macaroni, laughing with delight as she hears the sound it makes.

Diego, 2 years old, runs up a small grassy hill and rolls down. He gets up and does this again and again, laughing joyously as he rolls.

Jasmine, 3 years old, is at the easel carefully brushing paint over the entire surface of her forearm. She then moves the brush to her hand, painting each finger, covering the front, back, and nails.

Casey, 8 years old, and Randy, 13 years old, use the hose to create a giant mud puddle in the field behind the house. Both jump in joyfully, covering their entire bodies with the velvety muddy substance. They swish around a while, then jump out and spray each other off with icy water from the hose, squealing the entire time. Once clean, they jump right back in the mud and start over.

Re-Awakening Your Senses

As observations reveal, children explore the world with all of their senses, for learning and understanding, as well as for the absolute delight of a sensory experience. As a teacher, you must reawaken your senses to gain more understanding of children and increase your own pleasures and quality of life.

An effective starting place is naming what pleases you at a sensory level and describing what you like about it.

In *Art and Creative Development for Young Children* (Delmar, 1993), Robert Schirrmacher defines aesthetics as an abstract concept that means "perception" in Greek. Aesthetics, the author states,

An effective

starting place

is naming

what

pleases you

at a sensory level

and describing

what you like

about it.

are a focused and metaphorical way of knowing and experiencing the world, involving an attitude, process, and response to objects and experiences.

Appreciating aesthetics is a basic human response that involves active engagement, using all of the senses to ravish an object or experience. It allows us to become completely lost and totally consumed in the moment. Aesthetics include an awareness and appreciation of the natural beauty found in nature, art, movement, music, and life.

Cultivating your aesthetic sense will not only heighten your appreciation of how children approach the world, but also enrich your own life. Cultivating aesthetics may require shifting how you move through the world and what you pay attention to and focus on. Once the process begins, your life will be flooded with new awareness:

- You'll revel in the quality of light at different times of the day and seasons.
- You'll want to touch the weaving of colors in the coat next to you.
- Your ear will hear a bird song that leaves you smiling.
- A perfectly ripe piece of melon will make its way from your fingers, across your lips and tongue, leaving its delicious juice for you to savor.

Cultivating Aesthetics

It is worth studying Schirrmacher's discussion of the attitude, process, and responses to heighten your aesthetic sense. This study should involve not only your head but all of your senses. Consider the following.

The aesthetic *attitude* requires a willingness to stop and be involved in the present and approach experiences with openness and childlike freshness.

The aesthetic *process* involves intense focusing on the here and now; experiencing something as if for the very first time; listening attentively and getting lost in your senses; visually exploring and quietly contemplating; manipulating, feeling, touching; and taking time to be with an experience.

Your *response* to aesthetic experiences builds your understandings and enhances your quality of life. Notice your emotions: You may feel a sense of wonder, appreciation, joy, surprise, awe, exhilaration. Notice your physiological response: Are you smiling, perspiring, shivering, slumping, alert? Notice your mental response: Have you formed any new ideas from this experience?

Practicing with Watercolors

To practice the aesthetic attitude, process, and response, work with a set of watercolor paints, using the following guidelines:

- Visually explore and notice the colors, individually and as they mix together.
- Examine the effect that different amounts of water have on the color. Notice how water spreads the color on the paper.
- Experiment with different ways to use the brush. How many ways can you spread the paint?
- Use different techniques to move the color across the paper—splotches, dots, drops, lines, shapes.
- Take your time, watching what occurs with each of your explorations, becoming as engaged in the process as you can.
- Notice your emotions as you work. How are you feeling?
- Notice your physiological response. What is your body doing and saying to you?
- Notice your mental response. Do you have any new ideas? How would you evaluate this experience?

Notes

On Preparing Yourself

Use this space to record your thoughts about your personal journey toward becoming a responsive, child-centered practitioner.

What new roles would you like to try out?

Is there a disposition you want to enhance or try to replace in yourself?

How can you further cultivate your own sense of aesthetics, wonder, and joy in the world?

Look for Rikki Tikki
at All Times:
The True Story of the

Runaway Bunny

Sarah A. Felstiner,
Preschool Teacher

"To be with children is to work one-third with certainty and two-thirds with uncertainty and the new."
—*Loris Malaguzzi, founder of the Reggio Emilia schools*

When I begin a year of teaching, I have a choice of how to get from September to June. I can "drive," collecting maps and plotting my route by using lesson plans and a pre-formed curriculum. The journey for my class will be predictable—I know what ground we'll cover and what we'll encounter along the way. Driving will confine us to a chosen path, making impossible any turnoffs that are unpaved—essentially preventing the unplanned diversions that children, teachers, or parents discover.

Instead, I try to "fly," to rise higher for a different perspective and to lend the curriculum greater freedom of movement and direction. When I fly across the country, I may miss some of the details on the ground, but on the other hand, I'll get to appreciate the contours of the Grand Canyon, the tops of the mountains, the patchwork patterns of the fields. Educationally, I'm talking about the difference between a pre-planned, teacher-directed curriculum and one that is dynamic, experimental, and responsive to children's interests and needs.

My conviction of the need for an emergent curriculum was strengthened by my one-week visit to the remarkable preschools in Reggio Emilia, Italy. I had learned a great deal about these schools through articles, photos, slides, videos, and lectures by Reggio experts, and these encounters had me pretty convinced that "the Reggio approach" was an ideal way to teach young children. But when I visited Reggio

The teacher in this story describes her developmental process in learning to follow the children's lead for a meaningful curriculum to unfold.

Emilia, educators there helped me see that it is not enough to simply find and implement an approach that impresses you and suits your personal style. Instead, you must do as they do in Reggio: Make a commitment to *continually* question your techniques and philosophies through self-reflection, collaboration with your co-workers, and continual observation of the children you teach.

I knew that I couldn't and shouldn't try to replicate the Reggio schools, but I wanted to look for the pieces of their approach that would be meaningful to my teaching, and find ways to adapt those ideas for my use.

In that spirit, I returned to my classroom in California, determined to let children bring *their* ideas to the curriculum. I wanted each project, maybe even the whole year, to feel like one of those "teachable moments" where a child's genuine excitement becomes the basis for learning. This was my first step into emergent curriculum, filled with uncertainty and doubt, but eventually quite fulfilling. By the end of that school year, my experience with one runaway bunny had me completely convinced that the most genuine, effective, important curriculum in a preschool classroom is that which emerges from the needs and interests of the children.

Our pet rabbit, Rikki Tikki, was a much loved friend, and children in the class visited him daily in his large outdoor hutch. One Monday morning, however, we returned to school to find that the door of Rikki Tikki's cage had been pried open, and that our cherished friend was gone. Matt, the first child to wander over to say good morning to the rabbit, discovered the empty cage and immediately reported it to me. I was shocked and upset. How should a teacher respond to this news? How could she handle a situation like this? What does she say when Matt asks, "What happened?" Perhaps because of the strangeness of the situation, or perhaps due to the influence of my new Italian friends, or perhaps because I am, above all, honest with the children in my class, I responded, "I don't know." Then I listened to the children's ideas, using a tape recorder, camera, and paper and pens to document their words and images about what happened to Rikki Tikki.

The ideas came pouring out. Children speculated that coyotes had come to open the cage, or that Rikki Tikki had pushed his way out. Some thought he had gone to find some rabbit friends, some thought he was searching for his mother. Many children were convinced that he must still be somewhere in our yard. Because a few other outdoor items were strewn about the play yard, I thought perhaps the cage had been pried open by human visitors, but chose not to impose my hypothesis.

Children's ideas and suggestions were followed by actions. Some dug holes in the sand area and placed a piece of carrot at the bottom of each hole to lure Rikki Tikki back. Others built traps out of loose tires and climbing boards. Some began searching for clues with magnifying glasses and binoculars. Some were organizers: Jacqueline climbed to the top of the slide to call a meeting. Davis stood next to the empty cage and yelled, "Look for Rikki Tikki at all times!" Some children started drawing—signs, maps, clues, pictures of the missing rabbit—anything to help us find Rikki Tikki. But at the end of the first day, Rikki Tikki was still missing.

Over the next few weeks, many children used the paper and pens I brought outside each day. They drew elaborate maps that showed landmarks in our yard, footprints, and escape routes. They drew many pictures of Rikki Tikki, which they showed to parents, friends, and office staff, enlisting their help in the search. Writing skills blossomed as older children made signs that read "Lost rabbit" and "Thank you all for looking for Rikki Tikki," to post on the trees in our play yard. Some children wrote and drew letters for the rabbit and put them in a mailbox created just for Rikki Tikki. Even the youngest children began to add two long pointy ears to their basic scribbles and shapes. One small group collaborated on a flyer announcing the loss of our rabbit and describing his appearance. They made and colored multiple copies, posting them in and around the school.

Throughout this busy time, very few children even considered that we might not retrieve our rabbit. Stories like *The Runaway Bunny* and *Peter Rabbit* were read often, and came to have special meaning, perhaps because their rabbit protagonists return home in the end. For most children, it was just a question of looking hard enough, trying the right things, not giving up. Long after the adults inwardly considered the rabbit gone for good, children still searched for tracks, explored the yard, and took search parties to other classrooms. I supported and extended their ideas, providing the materials and supervision necessary for them to carry out their plans. Only after several weeks had passed did I begin to hear suggestions like "Maybe we should just get another bunny."

Then one morning in May, about a month after Rikki Tikki disappeared, I heard a rumor from another teacher that a parent in the school had seen our flyers, and had also seen a sign posted at another school across the street announcing a found rabbit. Doubting that Rikki Tikki might still be around a month later, and not wanting to raise hopes too high, one teacher and two children went across the street to investigate. They came back saying the rabbit looked awfully familiar. Another group went over with some drawings they had done and a photo of the rabbit to confirm his identity. In talking to the staff at the school across the street, I learned that they had been keeping him there for three weeks, and were just days away from taking him to the Humane Society. Word gradually spread among the children that Rikki Tikki had been found, and they got busy decorating his hutch with ribbons, paintings, and posters in preparation for his return. And of course they insisted that the broken door of his hutch be fixed.

The next morning, a small group of children set out with a carrying cage loaded on a red wagon. They crossed the street to the other school, lifted Rikki Tikki in, and wheeled him back. Before they even reached the door of the classroom, a crowd began to gather, and by the time they were all the way inside, the whole class was clustered around the small cage, calling to Rikki Tikki and touching his brown fur.

This incredible story of a real runaway bunny is what prompted me to analyze the ways I allow curriculum to develop in my classroom. I had to ask myself, "What if the pet rabbit doesn't escape next year? What if I don't even have a rabbit? How am I supposed to recreate that level of energy and engagement?" The experience with Rikki Tikki showed me that something special was happening in the classroom, and in thinking over the whole year, I realized that what I'd developed was a constant willingness to collaborate with the children. Through my efforts at letting the curriculum emerge from the children's interests, I had arrived at some basic guidelines for my teaching.

Honesty. I could have stifled the children's natural reactions and stunted their learning process by making up answers to their questions about Rikki Tikki's disappearance. I could have replaced him with a new rabbit right away, or claimed that he'd gone to "rabbit heaven." I could have diverted children's interest with unrelated songs and activities about bunnies, or distracted them with a different curriculum theme altogether. But instead I responded with honesty and genuine feeling, allowing their questions to guide our search.

Trust. I let the children be my guide. I followed at their pace, in the direction they wanted to go. It's adults, not children, who have the short attention span, I discovered. The children were willing to keep looking, keep working, and their involvement only grew deeper with each day that went by. I had lost faith, but the children never stopped believing they would find Rikki Tikki.

Responsiveness. Throughout the year, children learned that I was a valuable resource—that they could take the initiative and I would respond with eagerness. I was not so much a "teacher" but a co-learner and a fellow researcher. For me, that meant treating each new suggestion with some degree of seriousness, and trying to decide which ones were possible to pursue.

Risk. The Rikki Tikki project was a perfect demonstration of the axiom that the greatest risk brings the greatest reward. When I began to acknowledge that the children were guiding the curriculum, I felt both anxious and excited. For me, flying feels less safe than driving, perhaps because in flight I have to leave the reliable stability of the ground, and relinquish control of the pace and direction of travel. As a teacher, I feel this same risk when I abandon preset plans and expectations, allowing children to help steer the curriculum in new directions. In this case, there was certainly no guarantee that our hunt for Rikki Tikki would come to a happy end, but as a teacher I felt gratified when it did. On some cosmic level, I felt rewarded for pursuing this unplanned project and allowing it to fly. But actually, it doesn't matter whether the rabbit came back or not. The best thing I did for that group of children was to value their process, and to pay attention to what happened along the way.

Observation. I was a careful watcher and listener throughout the project. In addition to investigating the mystery at hand, I sought opportunities for each child to grow within this experience. New skills were developed, new leaders emerged, and social groups changed and expanded.

Documentation. I took many, many photographs, saved a lot of artwork, and continually wrote down children's words, because that documentation served as an ever-growing record of our search. In addition, my attention and record-keeping demonstrated to the children that I valued the work they were doing. At the same time, this documentation—compiled on a constantly changing bulletin board within the classroom—served to reassure parents that their children were busily working and playing and learning. Many parents became involved in the search and the saga, often bringing to school pictures and maps that children had made at home, or reporting new theories that had come up in family conversation. This was my evidence that the curriculum was expanding beyond the walls of the classroom, and that the children and I were becoming part of a learning community.

Collaboration. Collaboration among and between children, teachers, and parents was at the heart of all of this work. Collaboration requires *honesty*, *trust*, and *responsiveness*. Collaboration creates *risk*. But through *observation, documentation,* and *collaboration* with the children, I had one of the most successful teaching and learning experiences of my life.

I believe strongly that children deserve to be the authors of their own curriculum, but I still wish for more order and predictability than a truly emergent approach seems to provide. My struggle as a teacher is to find ways to make the work in my classroom feel both organized and spontaneous, both grounded and free. The compromise I've chosen is to promote emergent projects while carefully documenting children's work. By recording children's words, images, and activities, I not only facilitate their own learning, but I demonstrate to myself and to other adults the value of their emergent curriculum.

Recommended Resources

Throughout the early childhood profession, people are embracing variations of the child-centered, emergent approach to curriculum discussed in this handbook. Use the following resources as ongoing references. **The resources with an asterisk (*) are ones we find especially useful.**

Environments, Curriculum Planning, and Teacher Roles

* *Alerta: A Multicultural, Bilingual Approach to Teaching Young Children,* Leslie Williams and Yvonne De Gaetano (Reading, MA: Addison-Wesley, 1985). Provides a step-by-step guide for examining and reflecting on the lives and communities of children in your program. Includes many sample forms and lists to create a culturally relevant child care program.

Alike and Different: Exploring Our Humanity with Young Children, Bonnie Neugebauer, editor (Washington, DC: NAEYC, 1992, revised edition). A range of articles related to various aspects of diversity, including the needs of children, parents, and staff. Has practical ideas, including a checklist to use in evaluating children's books.

* *The Anti-Bias Curriculum: Tools for Empowering Young Children,* Louise Derman-Sparks (Washington, DC: NAEYC, 1989). Many valuable chapters on creating environments and practices that help children explore differences while avoiding the development of commonly held biases.

Back to the Basics, Bev Bos (Roseville, CA: Turn the Page Press, 1985). You will get a picture of the real basics of childhood from this book, which includes many examples to guide you through the pressure to have an earlier academic curriculum for children.

Beyond Dolls & Guns: 101 Ways to Help Children Avoid Gender Bias, Susan Hoy Crawford (Portsmouth, NH: Heinemann Educational Books, 1996). Though generally focused on school-aged children, there are still many excellent ideas to incorporate into programs for younger children.

Caring for Children in Family Child Care, D.G. Koralek, L. Colker, D.T. Dodge (Washington, DC: Teaching Strategies, 1993). A two-volume series with clear guidelines for keeping family child care organized and engaging for children.

The Creative Curriculum, Diane Trister Dodge (Washington, DC: Teaching Strategies, 1988). Excellent information and strategies for organizing a preschool environment into activity centers. Includes comprehensive lists of materials and equipment for each area and reasons why particular strategies for organizing are useful.

Diversity in the Classroom: A Multicultural Approach to the Education of Young Children, Frances E. Kendall (New York: Teachers College Press, 1983). One of the earlier and still most useful resources offering practical strategies for examining teachers' racial attitudes and the provisioning of a culturally sensitive classroom. Includes a valuable checklist for evaluating the classroom environment.

Dreamkeepers: Successful Teachers of African American Children, Gloria Ladson-Billings (San Francisco: Jossey-Bass Publishers, 1994). An important window into eight teachers who differ in style and methods but share an approach to teaching that affirms and strengthens cultural identity.

Educating Young Children, Mary Hohmann and David P. Weikart (Ypsilanti, MI: High/Scope Educational Research Foundation, 1995). This long-awaited update of *Young Children in Action* is a comprehensive guide to planning environments and a supportive climate for preschool-aged children. Includes practical information on how children construct knowledge and the role adults can play in this process. Whether or not you are interested in using the High/Scope Curriculum, this is a valuable resource for thinking about the basic elements of quality programming for young children.

* *Emergent Curriculum,* Elizabeth Jones and John Nimmo (Washington, DC: NAEYC, 1995). The story of professionals at a preschool program learning to work together to change their curriculum planning approach to an emergent, child-centered one. Many useful insights into translating the theory of a child-centered approach into practice. Probably one of the best resources for many of the ideas discussed in this handbook.

Engaging Children's Minds: The Project Approach, Lilian Katz and Sylvia Chard (Norwood, NJ: Ablex Publishing, 1993). You can adapt ideas from this book for preschool settings. This book includes important examples of the distinctions between a child-centered curriculum that engages children through projects and one that emphasizes memorization and recitation over thinking and inquiry.

Helping Children Love Themselves and Others: A Professional Handbook for Family Day Care, The Children's Foundation (Washington, DC: Children's Foundation, 1990). Focuses on anti-bias practices and equity issues, including an extensive list of children's books on these issues.

* *The Hundred Languages of Children: The Reggio Emilia Approach to Education,* Carolyn Edwards, Lella Gandini, and George Forman, editors (Norwood, NJ: Ablex Publishing, 1993, revised edition in press). A delicious look at what programs for young children are like when they spring from a culture that genuinely values children, families, teachers, and community. Wonderful examples of beauty and aesthetics in the environment. Includes a full discussion of representing children's lives and interests through documentation and display panels. Sees the teacher as curator, reconnaissance pilot, mentor, and collaborator.

* *The Play's the Thing: Teachers' Roles in Children's Play,* Elizabeth Jones and Gretchen Reynolds (New York: Teachers College Press, 1986). A terrific resource for understanding the importance of play and how to develop new roles and behaviors for child-centered curriculum. Includes examples of teacher representations of children's activities.

* *Prejudice: A Big Word for a Little Kid,* a video produced by Patty Johnson (St. Paul, MN: KSTP-TV). A compelling 20-minute tape with scenes and interviews depicting how quickly bias interweaves with identity development in young children. If you are unsure of the importance of anti-bias practices, watching this video will motivate you to learn how to implement them.

Room for Loving, Room for Learning: Finding the Space You Need in Your Family Child Care Home, Hazel Osborn (St. Paul, MN: Redleaf Press, 1994). Includes many inventive ideas to help you create better storage and activity areas in your home child care setting.

Scaffolding Children's Learning: Vygotsky and Early Childhood Education, Laura E. Berk and Adam Winsler (Washington, DC: NAEYC, 1995). This scholarly presentation of research and theory includes practical insights on teacher interventions that support children's learning efforts.

Serious Players in the Primary Classroom, Selma Wasserman (New York: Teachers College Press, 1992). This book is focused on older children, but offers valuable insight into why a play curriculum matches children's developmental needs and ways curriculum activities can be structured to promote curiosity and inquiry.

The Teacher's Idea Book: Daily Planning Around the Key Experiences, Michelle Grave (Ypsilanti, MI: High/Scope Press, 1989). You don't need to follow the official High/Scope approach to curriculum to benefit from the concrete ideas this book offers for hands-on learning activities. Familiarizing yourself with High/Scope's organization of developmental milestones into "key experiences" will enhance your ability to be articulate about the learning embedded in play.

Village of Kindness: Providing High-Quality Family Child Care, Joan Laurion (Madison, WI: University of Wisconsin School of Education, 1995). Written by a family child care provider to serve as a guide to a set of videos produced by Chip Donohue at the University of Wisconsin under the same name. Both are

same name. Both are excellent resources on the many different aspects of family child care and include stories from a diverse group of providers.

The Wonder of It: Exploring How the World Works, Bonnie Neugebauer, editor (Redmond, WA: Exchange Press, 1989, reissued in 1996). Full of terrific ideas and recommended materials to cultivate a sense of wonder and curiosity in young children.

Young Children: Active Learners in a Technological Age, June L. Wright and Daniel D. Shades, editors (Washington, DC: NAEYC, 1994). The discussion on using computers in a child-centered classroom is unique in that it is based on listening to children and observing their discoveries. Includes very practical ideas along with philosophical considerations.

Infants and Toddlers

Caring for Infants and Toddlers, Diane Trister Dodge, Amy Laura Dombro, and Derry Gosselin Koralek (Washington, DC: Teaching Strategies, 1991). A very practical guide for establishing programs for infants and toddlers. This book is well organized and readable, helping caregivers learn the "whys" of standard practices in quality caregiving.

Caring Spaces, Learning Places, Jim Greenman (Redmond, WA: Exchange Press, 1983). A wonderful look at creating environments for childhood, especially for infants and toddlers. The author inspires readers with quotes, stories, and strategies that reawaken the need for beauty and aliveness in programs for young children. There are also practical suggestions for design, organization, and storage.

Diary of a Baby, Daniel N. Stern, M.D. (New York: Harper Collins, 1990). With remarkable descriptions, the author describes ordinary experiences from the perspective of a baby. Eye-opening and engaging, this book helps readers to remember that adult perspectives are not always helpful to little ones.

* *Essential Connections: Ten Keys to Culturally Sensitive Child Care*, video (California Department of Education: Far West Laboratory Center for Child and Family Studies). An excellent overview of the elements of cultural difference that must be taken into account when providing care cross-culturally. Includes role plays for potential parent-caregiver cultural conflicts.

First Feelings, Stanley Greenspan, M.D., and Nora Thorndike (New York: Viking, 1989). A very useful text for understanding the developmental stages of young children's emotional growth.

* *Multicultural Issues in Child Care,* Janet Gonzalez-Mena (Mountain View, CA: Mayfield Publishing Company, 1993). An invaluable guide alerting us to cultural differences in perspectives and practices with regard to caring for young children. Examples of conflicts in daily routines and interactions are offered, along with guidelines for working through differences.

Prime Times: A Handbook for Excellence in Infant and Toddler Programs, Jim Greenman & Anne Stonehouse (St. Paul, MN: Redleaf Press, 1996). A long-awaited book by noted early childhood experts, this practical and thoughtful guide gives teachers and directors all of the information they need to establish high-quality programs for infants and toddlers.

* *Time With Toddlers,* a video produced by Margie Carter and Kidspace Child Care Center (distributed by Redleaf Press). With specific scenes of typical toddler behaviors and caregiving dilemmas, Margie guides the viewers in understanding, delighting in, and providing group care for this age group.

Observing Children

Bad Guys Don't Have Birthdays (1988); *Mollie is Three* (1986); and *Boys and Girls: Super Heroes in the Doll Corner* (1984); (Chicago, IL, University of Chicago Press). *The Boy Who Would be a Helicopter* (1990); *Kwanza and Me* (1995); *You Can't Say I Can't Play* (1992); and *White Teacher* (1979) all by Vivian Paley (Cambridge, MA: Harvard University Press).

A Guide to Observing and Recording Behavior, Warren Bentzen (Albany, NY: Delmar Publishers, 1993). An academic but valuable resource with an overview of developmental theories underlying approaches to observing, along with a detailed set of guidelines on observing and documenting.

The Logic of Action: Young Children at Work, Frances Pockman Hawkins (Boulder: Colorado Associated University Press, 1969). The author's close observations and detailed descriptions of deaf children illuminate our understanding of communication that goes beyond words.

Looking at Children's Play: A Bridge Between Theory and Practice, Patricia Monighann-Nourot, Barbara Scales, and Judith Van Hoorn (New York: Teachers College Press, 1987). Detailed descriptions of observing children's play, listening to parents, raising questions, and seeking answers.

Master Players, Elizabeth Jones and Gretchen Reynolds (New York: Teachers College Press, in press). Full of descriptive detail from masterful observers. Includes a review of a coding system to heighten your ability to interpret what you are seeing in children's play.

* The Portfolio and Its Use: Developmentally Appropriate Assessment of Young Children, Cathy Grace and Elizabeth F. Shores (Little Rock, AR: Southern Association on Children Under Six, 1992). One of the most useful resources available on developing a portfolio, work sample, and observation system to assess young children and effectively communicate with their families.

* Spreading the News: Sharing the Stories of Early Childhood, Margie Carter and Deb Curtis (St. Paul, MN: Redleaf Press, 1996). Offers detailed instructions and examples of how to observe children and create a story about what you understand about your observation. With full color examples, this little book is useful in learning to be an observer as well as creating visual displays that capture the attention of others.

Teacher, Sylvia Ashton-Warner (New York: Simon & Schuster, 1963). By now a classic, this book includes heartwarming stories and observations by a teacher of Maori children in Australia, all of which can be translated into practical strategies for preschool classrooms.

Observing the Natural World

Desert Notes, River Notes (New York: Avon Books, 1990) and *Field Notes* (New York: Alfred A Knopf, 1994) both by Barry Lopez. Lopez is a linguistic landscape artist who translates his observations into images you can feel on your skin.

* *Desert Quartet* (New York: Vintage Books, 1995) and
* *Refuge* (New York: Vintage Books, 1991) both by Terry Tempest-Williams. With captivating observations and descriptions of the birds, animals, and terrain of the desert canyons of Utah, the author provides a clear taste of living fully in the senses and body. In *Refuge,* her ideas become increasingly acute as she encounters the emotional terrain of watching her mother and grandmother die of cancer.

Diary of the Senses, Dianne Ackerman (New York: Vintage Books, 1990). The first in a series of books by the author, this book offers captivating descriptions of what our senses perceive.

Lives of a Cell, Lewis Thomas (New York: Bantam Books, 1979). Even if you have never thought of yourself as interested in science, the descriptions in this book will capture your imagination and desire to know more.

* *The Private Eye: Looking/Thinking by Analogy,* Kerry Ruef (Seattle, WA: The Private Eye Project, 1992). Great ideas for learning to observe as if for the first time. This is actually a K–12 curriculum that uses close observation with jeweler's loupes to think by analogy, write poetry, and theorize.

* *Solar Storms,* Linda Hogan (New York: Touchstone, 1995). The text of this story of three generations of native women living with a different way of seeing and knowing the world begs to be read aloud.

Professional Growth and Inspiration

In the Tiger's Mouth: An Empowerment Guide for Social Action, Katrina Shields (Philadelphia, PA: New Society Publishers, 1994). A practical yet inspiring workbook with self-guided activities to enhance working in groups to promote social change.

* Mentoring Curriculum: A Handbook for Mentors and Curriculum Guide for Trainers, National Center for the Early Childhood Work Force (Washington, DC: National Center for the Early Childhood Work Force, 1996). A mentor teacher system is one of the most promising efforts for professional development that rewards master teachers for staying in the classroom with children. This curriculum outlines the considerations, knowledge, and skills needed for mentoring relationships and systems.

* Speaking Out: Early Childhood Advocacy, Stacie G. Goffin and Joan Lombardi (Washington, DC: NAEYC, 1988). A terrific guide for the how and why of advocacy work in the early childhood field. Use it as a reference for child welfare, school reform, and worthy wages advocacy efforts.

* To Teach: The Journey of a Teacher, William Ayers (New York: Teachers College Press, 1993). A beautiful account of the mystery of teaching and the wonder of working with and learning from children. Both personally and professionally inspiring.

* Training Teachers: A Harvest of Theory and Practice, Margie Carter and Deb Curtis (St. Paul, MN: Redleaf Press, 1994). An in-depth discussion of the ideas of empowering education for adults and children, with scores of strategies for developing ourselves as effective teachers. A foundation for the ideas in *Reflecting Children's Lives.*

Montessori Schools
Though our approach to curriculum planning has fundamental differences, a visit to many Montessori classrooms reveals attention to presentation and aesthetics in materials and routines.

Schools of Reggio Emilia
There are international tours, study groups, newsletters, and books focused on this exemplary set of infant, toddler, and preschool programs in northern Italy. Currently, the Model Early Learning Center in Washington, DC, is the only Italian-accredited model in the United States. Coordination of information and related Reggio projects is handled by:

Reggio Children USA
1342 G Street NW, Suite 400
Washington, DC 20005-3105
(202) 265-9090

Waldorf Schools
Although we have no specific resource to recommend and there are significant differences in our approach from Waldorf Schools, we suggest that you visit a Waldorf classroom to see their practice of using toys and equipment made from natural materials and their attention to color, art, and aesthetics for children.

Personal Growth and Inspiration

For the Love of Children: Daily Affirmations for People Who Care for Children, Jean Steiner and Mary Steiner Whelan (St. Paul, MN: Redleaf Press, 1995). A gift to all teachers of young children, with short descriptions of the daily memorable incidents of our classrooms and inspiration to stretch for the dreams and recognition we long for.

Guide My Feet: Prayers and Meditations on Loving and Working For Children, Marian Wright Edelman (Boston, MA: Beacon Press, 1995). An important set of meditations for those struggling to care for and pass on values to young children. As with all of Edelman's work, there is wisdom, sound analysis, inspiration, and a call to action on behalf of children and our future.

Learning by Heart: Teaching to Free the Creative Spirit, Corita Kent and Jan Steward (New York: Bantam,1992). Lovely stories and specific exercises to jog you to re-animate your observing skills, curiosity, and artistic nature.

Uprooting Racism: How White People Can Work For Racial Justice, Paul Kivel (Philadelphia, PA: New Society Publishers, 1996). A thoughtful, useful workbook to assist

European Americans in better understanding the dynamics of racism, power, and privilege, and how to be an ally to people of color in transforming our society.

Useful Supplies

Catalogs for Loose Parts

* The Creation Station
7533 Olympic View Drive
Edmonds, WA 98026
(206) 775-7959

Creative Educational Surplus
9801 James Circle, Suite C
Bloomington, MN 55431
(612- 884-6427)

Music, Scarves, Dolls

For tapes, performances, and training using songs that reflect the lives of children, parents, and teachers, contact:

* The Song Growing Company, Tom Hunter
1225 East Sunset Drive, #518
Bellingham, WA 98226-3539
(360) 738-0340

For colorful, fluid, transparent scarves useful not only for movement and dancing with children, but also for adding a wonderful aesthetic quality to your environment, contact:

* Dancing Colors
PO Box 61
Langley, WA 98260-0061
(360) 221-5989

For multicultural, differently-abled, cross-generational dolls, especially suitable for adding "persona doll stories" to the life of your classroom, contact:

* People of Every Stripe
PO Box 12505
Portland, OR 97212
(503) 282-0612

Notes

About Resources

That You Find

Especially Useful

Use This Space For

Notes on Your Plans

for Discovering a

Curriculum That

Reflects Children's Lives

Other Publications From Redleaf Press

All the Colors We Are: The Story of How We Get Our Skin Color — Outstanding full-color photographs showcase the beautiful diversity of human skin color. Offers children a simple, accurate explanation.

The Kindness Curriculum: Introducing Young Children To Loving Values — Over 60 imaginative, exuberant activities that create opportunities for kids to practice kindness, empathy, conflict resolution, respect, etc.

Practical Solutions to Practically Every Problem: The Early Childhood Teacher's Manual — Over 300 proven developmentally appropriate solutions for all kinds of classroom problems.

Roots & Wings: Affirming Culture in Early Childhood Programs — A new approach to multicultural education that helps shape positive attitudes toward cultural differences.

Those Mean Nasty Dirty Downright Disgusting but...Invisible Germs — A delightful story that reinforces for children the benefits of frequent hand washing.

Training Teachers: A Harvest of Theory and Practice — Original strategies and training tools that bring a new approach to the *how* of teaching that supports great teacher development.

Transition Magician: Strategies for Guiding Young Children in Early Childhood Programs — Over 200 original, fun activities that help you magically turn transition times into calm, smooth activity changes.

For the Love of Children: Daily Affirmations for People Who Care for Children — An empowering book, yet warm and gentle. For those people who spend most of their waking hours caring for and about children.

Prime Times: A Handbook for Excellence in Infant and Toddler Programs — Guides you through the organization of a program of excellent care and education for infants and toddlers. Assists you in staffing the program with those who will maintain the vital quality of caregiving you establish.

Open the Door Let's Explore More! Field Trips of Discovery for Young Children — Filled with activities to do before, during and after delightful field trips. Reinforce learning while having fun.

So This Is Normal Too? Teachers and Parents Working Out Developmental Issues in Young Children — Makes the challenging behaviors of children vehicles for cooperation among adults and stepping stones to learning for children.